THE WOMEN

BY CLARE BOOTHE LUCE

★ Revised Edition

★

DRAMATISTS
PLAY SERVICE
INC.

THE WOMEN was first produced by Max Gordon at the Ethel Barrymore Theater, New York, December 26, 1936.

CHARACTERS

JANE

NANCY (*Miss Blake*)

PEGGY (*Mrs. John Day*)

SYLVIA (*Mrs. Howard Fowler*)

EDITH (*Mrs. Phelps Potter*)

MARY (*Mrs. Stephen Haines*)

MRS. WAGSTAFF

FIRST HAIRDRESSER

SECOND HAIRDRESSER

PEDICURIST

OLGA

EUPHIE

A MUD-MASK

COOK (*Ingrid*)

MISS FORDYCE

LITTLE MARY

MRS. MOREHEAD

FIRST SALESGIRL

SECOND SALESGIRL

HEAD SALESWOMAN (*Miss Shapiro*)

FIRST MODEL (*Miss Myrtle*)

SECOND SALESWOMAN

A FITTER

CORSET MODEL

PRINCESS TAMARA

CRYSTAL ALLEN

EXERCISE INSTRUCTRESS

MAGGIE

MISS TRIMMERBACK

MISS WATTS

A NURSE

LUCY

COUNTESS DE LAGE

MIRIAM AARONS

HELENE

FIRST CUTIE

SECOND CUTIE

FIRST SOCIETY WOMAN

SECOND SOCIETY WOMAN

SADIE

CIGARETTE GIRL

A DOWAGER

A DEBUTANTE

A GIRL IN DISTRESS

SYNOPSIS OF SCENES

Act I

Act II

THE WOMEN

ACT I

Scene 1

Mary Haines' living room. Today, Park Avenue living rooms are decorated with a significant indifference to the fact that ours is still a bi-sexual society. Period peacock alleys, crystal-hung prima-donna roosts, they reflect the good taste of their mistresses in everything but a consideration of the master's pardonable right to fit in his own home decor. Mary Haines' living room is not like that. It would be thought a comfortable room by a man. This, without sacrificing its own subtle, feminine charm. Above the fireplace there is a charming portrait of Mary's children—a girl of 11, a boy of 5 or 6. R., a door to the living quarters. L., another to the hall. C., a sofa, armchair, tea-table group, and in the good light from the window, a bridge-table group.

As curtain rises, Jane, a pretty and quite correct little Irish-American maid, is arranging the tea-table. Four women are playing bridge in a smoking-car cloud of smoke. They are:

Nancy, who is sharp, but not acid, sleek but not smart, a worldly and yet virginal 35. And her partner—

Peggy, who is pretty, sweet, 25. Peggy's character has not, will never quite "jell." And—

Sylvia, who is glassy, elegant, feline, 34. And her partner—

Edith, who is a sloppy, expensively dressed (currently, by Lane Bryant) matron of 33 or 34. Indifferent to everything but self, Edith is incapable of either deliberate maliciousness or spontaneous generosity.

SYLVIA. So I said to Howard, "What do you expect me to do?

5

Stay home and darn your socks? What do we all have money for? Why do we keep servants?"

NANCY. You don't keep them long, God knows— (*Placing pack of cards.*) Yours, Peggy.

PEGGY. Isn't it Mrs. Potter's? I opened with four spades. (*Sylvia firmly places pack before Peggy. Peggy, wrong again, deals.*)

SYLVIA. Second hand, you did. And went down a thousand. (*Patronizingly.*) Peggy, my pet, you can't afford it.

PEGGY. I can too, Sylvia. I'm not a pauper.

SYLVIA. If your bridge doesn't improve, you soon will be.

NANCY. Oh, shut up, Sylvia. She's only playing till Mary comes down.

SYLVIA. (*Querulously.*) Jane, what's Mrs. Haines doing upstairs?

JANE. (*Reproachfully.*) It's that lingerie woman *you* sent her, Mrs. Fowler.

SYLVIA. I didn't expect Mrs. Haines to buy anything. I was just trying to get rid of the creature. (*Jane exits.*) Peggy, bid.

PEGGY. Oh, mine? By.

SYLVIA. (*Looking at Peggy.*) She *won't* concentrate.

NANCY. She's in love, bless her. After the child's been married as long as you girls, she may be able to concentrate on vital matters like bridge.

SYLVIA. (*Bored.*) Another lecture on the Modern Woman?

NANCY. At the drop of a hat. By.

SYLVIA. I consider myself a perfectly good wife. I've sacrificed a lot for Howard Fowler—two spades. I devote as much time to my children as any of my friends.

NANCY. Except Mary.

SYLVIA. Oh, Mary, of course. Mary is an exception to all of us.

NANCY. Quite right. (*They are waiting for Peggy again.*) Peggy?

PEGGY. (*Uncertainly.*) Two no trumps? (*Edith rises suddenly. Plainly, she feels squeamish.*)

SYLVIA. (*Wearily.*) Edith, not *again*?

EDITH. Morning sickness! I heave the whole darn day. This is positively the last time I go through this lousy business for any man! Four spades. If men had to bear babies, there'd never be—

NANCY. —more than one child in a family. By. (*Edith sinks on edge of her chair, lays down cards.*)

PEGGY. I wish *I* were having a baby. We can't afford one now.

SYLVIA. And you'll never be able to, until you know Goren.

6

(*Arranging Edith's cards.*) Honestly, Edith! Why didn't you show a slam?

EDITH. (*Rising hurriedly.*) Oh, I *have* got to unswallow. Wait till you've had four, Peggy. You'd wish you'd never gotten past the bees and flowers. (*Exits precipitously.*)

NANCY. (*Disgusted.*) Poor, frightened, bewildered madonna!

SYLVIA. I'm devoted to Edith Potter. But she does get me down. You'd think she had a hard time. Dr. Briggs says she's like shelling peas. She ought to go through what *I* went through. Nobody knows!

NANCY. No clubs, partner?

SYLVIA. I had a Cæsarean. You should see my stomach— It's a slam!

NANCY. Are you sure?

SYLVIA. Got the king, Peggy? (*Peggy obligingly plays king.*) Thanks, dear, it's a slam. And the rubber. (*Rises, lights fresh cigarette, goes to armchair and perches.*) But I've kept my figure. I must say, I don't blame Phelps Potter for playing around.

PEGGY. Oh, does her husband . . . ?

SYLVIA. Oh, Phelps has made passes at all us girls. I do think it's bad taste for a man to try to make his wife's friends, *especially* when he's bald and fat. I told him once, "Phelps Potter," I said, "the next time you grab at me, I'm going straight to Edith."

NANCY. And did you?

SYLVIA. Certainly not. I wouldn't say anything to hurt Edith for the world. Besides, it isn't necessary. I'll say one thing for Edith. She's not as dumb as *some* of my friends. She's on to her husband.

PEGGY. (*Bravely.*) Do you think *he* is on to her?

SYLVIA. What do you mean?

PEGGY. If he could only hear her talk about him!

SYLVIA. Listen, Peggy, do we know how men talk about us when we're not around?

NANCY. I've heard rumors.

SYLVIA. Exactly. Peggy, you haven't been married long enough to form a realistic opinion of your husband.

PEGGY. Well, if I had one, I'd keep it to myself. Do you think I'd tell anybody in the world about the quarrels John and I have over money? I'd be too proud! (*Enter Edith. Goes to tea-table, gathers handful of sandwiches.*)

SYLVIA. All over, dear?

EDITH. Oh, that was a false alarm. What happened?

SYLVIA. Only a slam, dear. You do underbid.

EDITH. I'll bet you had me on the pan.

SYLVIA. I never say behind my friends' backs what I won't say to their faces. I said you ought to diet.

EDITH. There's no use dieting in my condition. I've got to wait until I can begin from scratch. Besides, I've got the most wonderful cook. She was with Mary. She said Mary let her go because she was too extravagant. I think this cook Mary has is too, too homey. (*Examines sandwich.*) Water cress. I'd just as soon eat my way across a front lawn.

SYLVIA. I think Mary's gone off terribly this winter. Have you noticed those deep lines here? (*Draws finger around her mouth.*)

NANCY. Smiling lines. Tragic, aren't they?

SYLVIA. Perhaps they *are*. Maybe a woman's headed for trouble when she begins to get too—smug.

NANCY. Smug? Don't you mean happy?

PEGGY. Mr. Haines adores her so!

SYLVIA. (*Flashing Edith a significant glance.*) Yes, doesn't he.

NANCY. (*Coldly.*) You just can't bear it, Sylvia, can you?

SYLVIA. Bear what?

NANCY. Mary's happiness. It gets you down.

SYLVIA. Nancy Blake, if there's one thing I can say for myself, I've never been jealous of another woman. Why should I be jealous of Mary?

NANCY. Because she's contented. Contented to be what she is.

SYLVIA. Which is what?

NANCY. A woman.

EDITH. And what, in the name of my revolting condition, am I?

NANCY. A female.

SYLVIA. Really. And what are you, pet?

NANCY. What nature abhors, I'm—a virgin—a frozen asset.

EDITH. I wish I were a virgin again. The only fun I ever had was holding out on Phelps. Nancy, you ought to thank God every night you don't have to make sacrifices for some man.

PEGGY. I wish I could make a little money, writing the way you do, Miss Blake.

NANCY. If you wrote the way I do, that's just what you'd make.

SYLVIA. You're not exactly a popular author, are you, dear?

8

NANCY. Not with you. Well, good news, Sylvia. My book is finished and once again I'm about to leave your midst.

PEGGY. Oh, I wish we could afford to travel. Where do you go this time, Miss Blake?

NANCY. Africa, shooting.

SYLVIA. Well, darling, I don't blame you. I'd rather face a tiger any day than the sort of things the critics said about your last book. (*Enter Mary. A lovely woman in her middle 30's. She is what most of us want our happily married daughters to be like. She is carrying several white boxes.*)

MARY. Sorry, girls. (*Teasing.*) Sylvia, must you always send me woebegone creatures like that lingerie woman? It's been a very expensive half hour for me.

PEGGY. (*Looking at Sylvia.*) For me too, Mrs. Haines.

MARY. (*Laughing.*) Nonsense, Peggy, you were playing for me. Here. (*Hands Peggy a box.*) Don't open it now. It's a bed-jacket. Or a tea cozy. Or something padded. I wouldn't know. I was crying so hard.

SYLVIA. You didn't believe that woman's sob story?

MARY. Of course I did. (*She really didn't.*) Anyway, she's a lot worse off than you and I. (*Putting down another box.*) Edith, wee garments—

EDITH. Darling, how sweet! (*It comes over her again.*) Oh, my God! I'm sick as a cat. (*Sits.*)

SYLVIA. It's a girl. Girls always make you sicker.

NANCY. Even before they're born?

EDITH. I don't care what it is. I've lost everything including my curiosity. Why did God make it take nine months?

NANCY. (*Helpfully.*) It takes an elephant seven years.

EDITH. I wish I were an elephant. I'll look like one anyway before I'm finished. And it would be heaven not to worry for seven years.

MARY. (*Laughing.*) Oh, Edith, it is rather trying. But when it's all over, isn't it the grandest thing in the world to have them?

JANE. (*Entering with tea-kettle.*) Ma'am, Mr. Haines would like to speak to you on the phone.

MARY. Oh, I can feel what it is in my bones, Jane. (*To others.*) Stephen's going to be kept at the office again tonight. (*Exits.*)

SYLVIA. Give him my love, pet.

MARY. (*Off stage.*) I will.

9

SYLVIA. (*She never lets anything pass.*) Nancy, you couldn't be more wrong about me and Mary.

NANCY. Still rankling?

SYLVIA. Jealous? As a matter of fact, I'm sorry for her.

NANCY. Oh-ho? Why?

SYLVIA. (*Mysteriously.*) Well, for all *we* know she may be living in a fool's paradise with Stephen.

NANCY. Let's check that one for a moment, Sylvia. Jane, are the children in?

JANE. Yes, Miss. Just back from the Park. (*Edith rises—Sylvia, in pantomime, signals her not to leave the room. This is not lost on Nancy. For a moment she hesitates at door.*)

PEGGY. Oh, I'd love to see Mrs. Haines' little girl, Miss Blake—

NANCY. (*Following Peggy.*) Come along, child. Anyway, it's our turn to go on the pan. But we don't have to worry. You've got a poor man. I've got no man at all. (*They exit.*)

EDITH. (*Goes to tea-table—pours 2 cups. Jane empties ash trays.*) This is positively the last time I play bridge with Nancy. She never misses a chance to get in a dig. What has a creature like her got but her friends? (*Jane exits, closing door, L. Sylvia stealthily closes door, R.*) The way she kept at you about Mary made me so nervous, I thought I'd scream. And in my condition—

SYLVIA. Edith, I've got to tell you! I'll burst if I wait!

EDITH. I *knew* you had something! (*She brings her well-laden plate and tea-cup and settles herself happily beside Sylvia on sofa.*)

SYLVIA. You'll die! Stephen Haines is cheating on Mary!

EDITH. I don't believe you; is it true?

SYLVIA. Wait till you hear. (*Now she is into it.*) You know I go to Michael's for my hair. You ought to go, pet. I despise whoever does yours. Well, there's the most wonderful new manicurist there. (*Shows her scarlet nails.*) Isn't that divine? Jungle Red—

EDITH. Simply divine. Go on.

SYLVIA. It all came out in the most extraordinary way, this morning. I tried to get you on the phone—

EDITH. I was in the tub. Go on.

SYLVIA. This manicurist, she's marvelous, was doing my nails. I was looking through *Vogue*, the one with Mary in the Junior League Ball costume—

EDITH. —in that white wig that flattered her so much?

SYLVIA. (*Nodding.*) Well, this manicurist: "Oh, Mrs. Fowler," she says, "is that that Mrs. Haines who's so awfully rich?"

EDITH. Funny how people like that think people like us are awfully rich.

SYLVIA. I forget what she said next. You know how those creatures are, babble, babble, babble, babble, and never let up for a minute! When suddenly she says: "I know the girl who's being *kept* by Mr. Haines!"

EDITH. No!

SYLVIA. I swear!

EDITH. (*Thrilled.*) Is she someone *we* know?

SYLVIA. No! That's what's so awful about it. She's a friend of this manicurist. Oh, it wouldn't be so bad if Stephen had picked someone in his own class. But a blond floosie!

EDITH. But how did Stephen ever meet a girl like that?

SYLVIA. How do men ever meet girls like that? That's what they live for, the rats!

EDITH. But—

SYLVIA. I can't go into all ..ie details now. They're utterly fantastic—

EDITH. You suppose Mary knows?

SYLVIA. No. Mary's the kind who couldn't help showing it if she knew.

EDITH. (*Nodding, her mouth full of her third cake.*) She has no self-control. Well, she's bound to find out. If a woman's got any instincts, she feels when her husband's off the reservation. I know *I* would.

SYLVIA. Of course you would, darling. Not Mary— (*Rises, walks about, wrestling with Mary's sad problem.*) If only there were some way to *warn* her!

EDITH. (*Horrified, following her.*) Sylvia! You're not going to tell her?

SYLVIA. Certainly not. I'd *die* before I'd be the one to hurt her like that!

EDITH. Couldn't someone shut that manicurist up?

SYLVIA. A good story like that? A lot girls like that care whose life they ruin.

EDITH. *Isn't* it a dirty trick?

SYLVIA. Isn't it *foul?* It's not as though only Mary's friends knew. We could keep our mouths shut.

11

EDITH. I know plenty that I never *breathe* about my friends' husbands!

SYLVIA. So do I! (*They exchange a sudden glance of sharp suspicion.*) Anyway, the whole thing's disgustingly unfair to Mary. I feel absolutely sick about it, just knowing about it—

EDITH. I adore Mary—

SYLVIA. I *worship* her. She's my dearest friend in all the world— (*Voices off stage. They sit down at card-table and begin to play solitaire hastily. Enter Nancy and Peggy.*)

NANCY. Well, Sylvia, feeling better?

SYLVIA. (*Innocently.*) Meaning what?

NANCY. Must've been a choice piece of gossip. You both look so *relaxed.*

SYLVIA. Nancy, were you listening at that door?

PEGGY. Oh, Mrs. Fowler, we were in the nursery. (*Mary enters.*)

SYLVIA. (*Quickly.*) Well, darling, how is Stephen, the old dear? And did you give him my love?

MARY. I did. Stephen's not so well, Sylvia.

SYLVIA. Oh? What's the trouble?

MARY. Nervous indigestion. That's why I have such a plain cook now.

EDITH. Phelps has had indigestion for years. You should hear that man rumble in the night. Like a truck on cobblestones.

SYLVIA. There's nothing—worrying Stephen?

MARY. Oh, no, he's just been working too hard. He's not coming home tonight.

SYLVIA. Are you sure it's *work*, darling, and not a beautiful blonde?

MARY. Stephen? (*Laughing, and perhaps a little smugly, too.*) Oh, Sylvia.

EDITH. (*Afraid Sylvia will go too far.*) Sylvia, let's play another rubber.

SYLVIA. Stephen's a very attractive man.

MARY. Isn't he? I can't imagine why he hasn't deserted me for some glamorous creature long ago.

NANCY. (*Alarmed.*) Mary, you *do* sound smug.

MARY. Oh, let me be, Nancy. How can you be too sure of what you believe in most?

SYLVIA. I wouldn't be sure of the Apostle Paul. I always tell

12

Howard, "If you ever manage to make a fool of me, I'll deserve what I get."

NANCY. You certainly will. (*Faces Sylvia squarely.*) Now, Sylvia, let's have it.

SYLVIA. Have what?

NANCY. Just what did you mean when you said Mary was living in a fool's paradise?

MARY. What?

SYLVIA. (*Angrily.*) Nancy, don't be absurd. (*A pause. Then, wriggling out of it.*) Oh, Mary, I was just trying to make a typical Nancy Blake wisecrack about marriage. I said, "A woman's paradise is always a fool's paradise!"

MARY. That's not bad, is it, Nancy? Well, Sylvia, whatever I'm living in, I like it. Nancy, cut.

SYLVIA. (*Sylvia examines her nails minutely, suddenly shows them to Mary.*) Mary, how do you like my new polish?

NANCY. (*Not looking.*) Too, too—too!

SYLVIA. You can't imagine how it stays on. I get it at Michael's—There's a terrific new manicurist there—

EDITH. (*Protestingly.*) Oh, Sylvia—

SYLVIA. Olga's her name. She's out of this world.

EDITH. Will you cut, Sylvia?

SYLVIA. It's called Jungle Red.

NANCY. Just the thing for tearing your friends apart.

SYLVIA. I'll be damned, Nancy, if I'll let you ride me any more!

MARY. Now, Sylvia, Nancy's just being clever too.

SYLVIA. She takes a crack at everything about me. Even my nails!

MARY. (*Laughing.*) Well, I like it. I really do! It's new and chic. (*Pats her hand.*) Michael's, Olga, Jungle Red? I'll remember that. (*Cuts cards.*) You and I, Sylvia. I feel lucky today.

SYLVIA. (*With a sweet, pitying smile.*) Do you, darling? Well, you know what they say, "Lucky in cards—"

CURTAIN

ACT I

SCENE 2

An afternoon, a few days later. A hairdressing booth in Michael's. An elegantly functioned cubbyhole. R., a recessed mirror in wall. L., from high partition pole, a curtain to floor. Rear wall is a plain partition. C., swivel hairdressing chair. Above it from an aluminum tree, the hanging thicket of a permanent-wave machine. In wall, gadgets for curling irons, electric outlets which connect with wires to drying machine, hand drier, manicurists' table-light, stools for pedicurists, and manicurist, Olga.
As curtain rises, the booth is, to put it mildly, full.
The Countess de Lage, an amiable, silly, fat and forty heiress-type, is in chair, having her hair dyed.
Olga, at her R., is doing her nails. Her fat bare feet rest in the lap of the Pedicurist. 1st Hairdresser applies the dye. 2nd Hairdresser, watch in hand, times the operation. The Countess, apparently inured to public execution, smokes, reads magazine on her lap, occasionally nibbles a sandwich which Olga passes her from a tray near her instruments.

COUNTESS. That stuff is burning my scalp! Mon Dieu! (*Pronounced Mon Doo.*)
2ND HAIRDRESSER. Be brave! One minute more!
COUNTESS. (*In pain.*) O-o-oo!
1ST HAIRDRESSER. It's going to be so worth it, Countess.
COUNTESS. It's dribbling down my neck!
2ND HAIRDRESSER. Be brave!
COUNTESS. O-o-o-o! My nerves— Oo—my God! (*To Pedicurist.*) My sandwich— (*Olga hands her sandwich.*)
2ND HAIRDRESSER. Ten seconds. We must suffer to be beautiful. (*Curtain parts, a figure in flowing white half-enters. It is, judging by the voice, a woman, but its face is completely obliterated by a mud-mask.*)
MUD-MASK. Whoops!—I thought I was in here. Why, hiya, Countess de Lage. (*Coyly.*) Guess who I am? (*A second face ap-*

14

pears over this intruder's shoulder. At first, it looks like another mud-mask. It's not. It's the colored maid, Euphie. She clutches the shoulder of the mud-mask.)

EUPHIE. Mustn't talk, Miss Aarons. You'll crack your mud-mask.

MIRIAM. I was half-cracked to let you put this glop on me. (Exit followed by Euphie.)

COUNTESS. Who was that?

1ST HAIRDRESSER. Miriam Aarons.

COUNTESS. Who?

1ST HAIRDRESSER. Miriam Aarons. She's playing in "The Vanities."

COUNTESS. Does she know me?

OLGA. Oh, everybody knows you, Countess de Lage. (Full of awe.) You're in the society columns almost every day.

COUNTESS. Miriam Aarons? It's a funny thing about me. I have no memory for names or faces. Well, I suppose she came to one of my parties. I never know who the Count's going to ask. For an aristocrat, mon dieu, is he democratic!

OLGA. I've seen pictures of the Count. He's awful handsome . . .

COUNTESS. (Thoughtfully.) What does a mud mask do for you?

1ST HAIRDRESSER. Tightens the chin and throat muscles.

2ND HAIRDRESSER. Brings on a natural glow—

PEDICURIST. Miriam Aarons has lovely skin.

1ST HAIRDRESSER. Not lovelier than yours, Countess!

1ST, 2ND HAIRDRESSERS, PEDICURIST, OLGA. (In fawning chorus:) Oh, yours is lovely. Why, not nearly as lovely. You have lovely skin.

COUNTESS. I do think it's rather good for a woman my age!

1ST HAIRDRESSER. You mustn't talk as if you were an old woman, Countess dear!

COUNTESS. (Lying.) After all, I'm 45.

1ST HAIRDRESSER. Mustn't tell anyone.

2ND HAIRDRESSER. You don't look a day over 40.

CHORUS OF HAIRDRESSERS, PEDICURIST, OLGA. You look so young! Why not a day . . . ! You certainly don't look your age. Not a day over 40!

1ST HAIRDRESSER. Haven't you slimmed down since last year?

COUNTESS. (With satisfaction.) My last divorce took off ten pounds. (A pause.) I think I'll have a mud mask.

15

1ST HAIRDRESSER. (*To 2nd Hairdresser.*) Tell the desk Countess de Lage is working in a mud. (*Exit 2nd Hairdresser.*)

COUNTESS. (*Admiring her nail polish on one hand.*) Tres gai, n'est-ce pas?

OLGA. Oh, no, we don't have "tray gay." That's Jungle Red. Everybody's wild about it. Mrs. Howard Fowler wears it. You know Mrs. Fowler—the best dressed woman in New York?

1ST HAIRDRESSER. (*To Countess.*) There, dear. The agony's over! We'll move to the shampoo. (*Calling off.*) Euphie! Clear this booth.

PEDICURIST. (*Rising, gathering up her pedicure basket, and the Countess' stockings.*) We won't put your stockings on yet, Countess. We don't want to smear your beautiful big toe. (*Pedicurist and Hairdresser help Countess to her feet. Countess, leaning on their arms, has to walk on her heels, her toes still wadded with cotton.*)

COUNTESS. (*Singing.*) Allons enfants de la patrie! On to the mud mask! (*Euphie opens curtain. 1st Hairdresser, Pedicurist, Countess exit. During the ensuing dialogue Euphie cleans the floor of the booth with a long-handled sweeper, brush and pan, and Olga puts manicure things away in her basket.*)

OLGA. That old gasoline truck! Fifty-two, if she's a day. One more permanent and she won't have a hair left on her head!

EUPHIE. (*Viewing dustpan.*) She sure does shed.

OLGA. I'll bet this husband sheds her in a year. A woman is a fool to marry a man ten years younger. Know what I heard a client under the dryer tell a friend? The Count's a pansy! (*Olga exits, pantomiming "pansy." Enter 2nd Hairdresser.*)

2ND HAIRDRESSER. Countess de Lage forgot her bag. (*She retrieves the bag from the floor. It is open. She is about to close it. Looks in. Laughs. Pulls out a leather whiskey flask, shows it without comment to Euphie, then drops it back in bag, and exits. Euphie starts to follow, then holds back curtain. Enter Mary, followed by Nancy.*)

MARY. (*To Euphie.*) Thank you.

EUPHIE. Yes Ma'am. (*Exits.*)

MARY. (*To Nancy.*) So, as I say, I woke up this morning, and for no good reason I felt the time has come to change my hairdo— (*Enter 2nd Hairdresser.*)

16

2ND HAIRDRESSER. Mr. Michael will be ten minutes, madam. Anyone in particular for your manicure?

MARY. I'd like the girl who does Mrs. Fowler's nails.

2ND HAIRDRESSER. Olga. I'll see. (*Exits.*)

NANCY. God, I'd love to do Mrs. Fowler's nails, right down to the wrist, with a nice big buzz saw.

MARY. Sylvia's all right. She's a good friend underneath.

NANCY. Underneath what?

MARY. Nancy, you don't humor your friends enough.

NANCY. So that's the big idea coming here? You're humoring Sylvia?

MARY. Oh, you did hurt her. I had it all over again at lunch. (*She catches a glimpse of herself in mirror.*) Nancy, am I getting old?

NANCY. Who put that in your head? Sylvia?

MARY. Tell me the truth.

NANCY. Beauty is in the eye of the beholder, and twaddle to that effect.

MARY. But it's such a scary feeling when you see those little wrinkles creeping in.

NANCY. Time's little mice.

MARY. And that first gleam of white in your hair. It's the way you'd feel about autumn, if you knew there'd never be another spring—

NANCY. (*Abruptly.*) There's only one tragedy for a woman.

MARY. Growing old?

NANCY. Losing her man.

MARY. That's why we're all so afraid of growing old.

NANCY. Are you afraid?

MARY. Well, I was very pretty when I was young. I never thought about it twice then. Now I know it's why Stephen loved me.

NANCY. Smart girl.

MARY. Now I think about it all the time.

NANCY. Love is not love which alters when it alteration finds. Shakespeare.

MARY. Well, he told me, on my birthday, I'd always look the same to him.

NANCY. Nice present. No jewels?

MARY. It rained that day. He brought me a bottle of perfume called "Summer Rain."

17

NANCY. How many ounces?

MARY. Nancy, you've never been in love.

NANCY. Says who?

MARY. (*Surprised.*) Have you?

NANCY. Yes.

MARY. You never told me.

NANCY. You never asked— (*Wistfully.*) Neither did he. (*Olga enters with fresh bowl of water.*) Here, innocent. (*Gives book to Mary.*) The book my readers everywhere have been waiting for with such marked apathy.

MARY. "All the Dead Ladies"?

NANCY. Originally called, "From the Silence of the Womb." My publisher thought that would make too much noise.

MARY. What's it about? (*Olga begins to file Mary's nails.*)

NANCY. Women I dislike: "Ladies—"

MARY. Oh, Nancy!

OLGA. (*Putting Mary's hand in water.*) Soak it, please.

NANCY. No good? Too bad. It's a parting shot. I'm off.

MARY. Off?

NANCY. Africa.

MARY. But not today?

NANCY. I knew if I told you you'd scurry around and do things. A party. Steamer baskets of sour fruit. Not nearly as sour as the witty cables your girl friends would send me— So don't move. No tears. For my sake—just soak it. Good-bye, Mary—

MARY. Good-bye, Nancy. I'll miss you.

NANCY. I doubt it. Practically nobody ever misses a clever woman. (*Exits.*)

OLGA. Funny, isn't she?

MARY. She's a darling.

OLGA. She's a writer? How do those writers think up those plots? I guess the plot part's not so hard to think up as the end. I guess anybody's life'd make a interesting plot if it had a interesting end— Mrs. Fowler sent you in? (*Mary, absorbed in Nancy's book, nods.*) She's sent me three clients this week. Know the Countess de Lage? Well, she inherited this fortune when her first husband died and—

MARY. (*Shortly.*) I don't know her—

OLGA. Soak it, please. Know Mrs. Potter?

MARY. Yes.

18

OLGA. She's pregnant again.

MARY. (*She wants to read.*) I know.

OLGA. Soak it, please. (*Puts Mary's hand in water. Begins on other hand.*) Know Mrs. Stephen Haines?

MARY. I certainly do—

OLGA. I guess Mrs. Fowler's told you about her! Mrs. Fowler feels awfully sorry for her.

MARY. (*Laughing.*) Oh, she does! Well, I don't. I—

OLGA. You would if you knew this Crystal Allen.

MARY. Crystal Allen?

OLGA. Yes, you know. The girl who's living with Mr. Haines? (*Mary starts violently.*) Don't you like the file? Mrs. Potter says it sets her unborn child's teeth on edge.

MARY. (*Indignant.*) Whoever told you such a thing?

OLGA. Oh, I thought you knew. Didn't Mrs. Fowler—?

MARY. No—

OLGA. Then you will be interested. You see, Crystal Allen is a friend of mine. She's really a terrible man-trap. Soak it, please. (*Mary, dazed, puts her hand in the dish.*) She's behind the perfume counter at Saks'. So was I before I got fi—left. That's how she met him.

MARY. Met Stephen Haines?

OLGA. Yeah. It was a couple of months ago. Us girls weren't busy. It was an awful rainy day, I remember. So this gentleman walks up to the counter. He was the serious type, nice-looking, but kind of thin on top. Well, Crystal nabs him. "I want some perfume," he says. "May I awsk what type of woman for?" Crystal says, very ritzy. That didn't mean a thing. She was going to sell him our feature, Summer Rain, anyway. "Is she young?" Crystal says. "No," he says, sort of embarrassed. "Is she the glamorous type?" Crystal says. "No, thank God," he says. "Thank God?" Crystal says and bats her eyes. She's got those eyes which run up and down a man like a searchlight. Well, she puts perfume on her palm and in the crook of her arm for him to smell. So he got to smelling around and I guess he liked it. Because we heard him tell her his name, which one of the girls recognized from Igor Cassini's column— Gee, you're nervous— Well, it was after that I left. I wouldn't of thought no more about it. But a couple of weeks ago I stopped by where Crystal lives to say hello. And the landlady says she'd moved to the kind of house where

19

she could entertain her gentleman friend— "What gentleman friend?" I says. "Why, that Mr. Haines that she's had up in her room all hours of the night," the landlady says— (*Mary draws her hand away.*) Did I hurt?

MARY. No. But I don't really need a manicure.

OLGA. Just polish? One coat, or two? (*Picks up a red bottle.*)

MARY. None. (*Rises, goes to chair, where she left her purse.*)

OLGA. But I thought that's what you came for? All Mrs. Fowler's friends—

MARY. I think I've gotten what all Mrs. Fowler's friends came for. (*Puts dollar bill on table.*)

OLGA. (*Picks up bill.*) Oh, thanks— Well, good-bye. I'll tell her you were in, Mrs.—?

MARY. Mrs. Stephen Haines.

OLGA. Mrs.—? Oh, gee, gee! Gee, Mrs. Haines—I'm sorry! Oh, isn't there something I can do?

MARY. Stop telling that story!

OLGA. Oh, sure, sure, I will!

MARY. And please don't tell anyone— (*Her voice breaks.*) that you told it to *me*—

OLGA. Oh, I won't, gee, I promise! Gee, that would be kind of humiliating for you! (*Defensively.*) But in a way, Mrs. Haines, I'm kinda *glad* you know. Crystal's a terrible girl—I mean, she's terribly clever. And she's terribly pretty, Mrs. Haines—I mean, if I were you I wouldn't waste no time getting Mr. Haines away from her— (*Mary turns abruptly away.*)

MARY. Thank you. Goodday. (*Olga eyes bill in her hand distastefully, suddenly puts it down on table and exits. Mary, alone, stares blankly in mirror, then, suddenly focusing on her image, leans forward, searching her face between her trembling hands. A drier goes on in next booth. A shrill voice rises above its drone.*)

VOICE. —Not too hot! My sinus! So *she* said: "I wouldn't want anybody in the world to know," and *I* said: "My dear, you know you can trust *me!*"

CURTAIN

ACT I

SCENE 3

An hour later. Mary's boudoir. Charming, of course. A door to bedroom, R. A door to hall, L. A chaise-longue, next to it, a table with books, flowers, a phone. A dressing table.

As curtain rises, Mary is discovered on chaise-longue, twisting a damp handkerchief in her hands. Jane enters from hall, carrying a tea tray.

JANE. You looked like you needed a cup of tea when you came in, ma'am.

MARY. I do. I have a sudden headache. And, Jane—my mother will be here in a few minutes. A cup for her.

JANE. Yes, ma'am. (*Enter Miss Fordyce. She is a raw-boned, capable English spinster of 32.*)

MISS FORDYCE. May I see you, Mrs. Haines?

MARY. Of course, Miss Fordyce.

MISS FORDYCE. It's about little Mary— Really, Mrs. Haines, you'll have to talk to your child. She's just smacked her little brother, hard. Pure temper.

MARY. What did little Stevie do to her, Miss Fordyce?

MISS FORDYCE. Well, you see, it happened while I was down getting my tea. When I came up, she'd had such a tantrum, she'd made herself ill. She positively refuses to discuss the incident with me. But I'm quite sure the dear boy hadn't done a thing.

MARY. You're very apt to take the boy's side, Miss Fordyce.

MISS FORDYCE. Not at all. But in England, Mrs. Haines, our girls are not so wretchedly spoiled. After all, this *is* a man's world. The sooner our girls are taught to accept the fact *graciously*—

MARY. (*Gently.*) Send her in to me, Miss Fordyce. (*Exit Miss Fordyce.*) Oh, Jane, I don't understand it. Miss Fordyce really prefers Mary, but she insists we all make a little god of Stevie. (*Exits to bedroom, leaving door open.*)

JANE. Them English ones always stand up for the boys. But they say since the War, ma'am, there's six women over there to every man. Competition is something fierce! Over here, men aren't so scarce. You can treat them the way they deserve— (*Enter little*

Mary. She is a broad-browed, thoughtful, healthy little girl, physically well developed for her age.)

LITTLE MARY. Where's Mother?

JANE. You're going to catch it. Smacking your little brother. *(Mimicking Miss Fordyce.)* Such a dear, sweet little lad—shame. *(Little Mary does not answer.)* I'll bet you wish you were Mother's girl, instead of Daddy's girl today, don't you? *(Little Mary doesn't answer.)* What's the matter, the cat got your tongue? *(Enter Mary, wearing negligee.)*

MARY. Hello, darling— Aren't you going to kiss me? *(Little Mary doesn't move.)* What red eyes!

LITTLE MARY. I was mad. I threw up. When you throw up, doesn't it make you cry?

MARY. *(Smiling.)* Stevie tease you? *(Little Mary, embarrassed, looks at Jane. Jane snickers, takes hint and goes out.)* Well, darling?

LITTLE MARY. Mother, I don't know how to begin.

MARY. *(Sitting on chaise-longue, and putting out her hand.)* Come here. *(Little Mary doesn't budge.)* Would you rather wait until tonight and tell Dad?

LITTLE MARY. *(Horrified.)* Oh, Mother, I couldn't tell him! *(Fiercely.)* And I'd be killed to death before I'd tell skinny old Miss Fordyce—

MARY. That's not the way for my dear little girl to talk.

LITTLE MARY. *(Setting her jaw.)* I don't want to be a dear little girl. *(She suddenly rushes to Mary's outstretched arms in tears.)* Oh, Mother dear, Mother dear!

MARY. Baby, what?

LITTLE MARY. What brother said!

MARY. What did he say, the wretched boy?

LITTLE MARY. *(Disentangling herself.)* He said I had bumps!

MARY. Bumps? You don't mean mumps?

LITTLE MARY. No, bumps. He said I was covered with disgusting bumps!

MARY. *(Alarmed.)* Mary, where?

LITTLE MARY. *(Touching her hips and breasts with delicate, ashamed finger tips.)* Here and here!

MARY. Oh— *(Controlling her relieved laughter, and drawing little Mary to her side.)* Of course you have bumps, darling. Very pretty little bumps. And you have them because—you're a little girl.

LITTLE MARY. (*Wailing.*) But, Mother dear. I don't want to be a little girl. I hate girls! They're so silly, and they tattle, tattle—

MARY. Not really, Mary.

LITTLE MARY. Yes, Mother, I know. Oh, Mother, what *fun* is there to be a lady? What can a lady do?

MARY. (*Cheerfully.*) These days, darling, ladies do all the things men do. They fly aeroplanes across the ocean, they go into politics and business—

LITTLE MARY. *You* don't, Mother.

MARY. Perhaps I'm happier doing just what I do.

LITTLE MARY. What do you do, Mother?

MARY. Take care of you and Stevie and Dad.

LITTLE MARY. You don't, Mother. Miss Fordyce and the servants do.

MARY. (*Teasing.*) I see. I'm not needed around here.

LITTLE MARY. (*Hugging her.*) Oh, Mother, I don't mean that. It wouldn't be any fun at all without *you*. But, Mother, even when the ladies *do* do things, they stop it when they get the lovey-dovies.

MARY. The what?

LITTLE MARY. Like in the movies, Mother. Ladies always end up so *silly*. (*Disgusted.*) Lovey-dovey, lovey-dovey all the time!

MARY. Darling, you're too young to understand—

LITTLE MARY. But, Mother—

MARY. "But Mother, but Mother!" There's one thing a woman can do, no man can do.

LITTLE MARY. (*Eagerly.*) What?

MARY. Have a child. (*Tenderly.*) Like you.

LITTLE MARY. Oh, that! Everybody knows that. But is that any fun, Mother dear?

MARY. Fun? No. But it is—joy. (*Hugging her.*) Of a very special kind.

LITTLE MARY. (*Squirming away.*) Well, it's never sounded specially exciting to me— I love you, Mother. But I bet you anything you like, Daddy has more *fun* than you! (*She slips away from Mary. Then sees Mary's dispirited face, turns and kisses her warmly.*) Oh, I'm sorry, Mother. But you just *don't understand!* (*A pause.*) Am I to be punished, Mother?

MARY. (*She is thinking about something else.*) What do you think?

LITTLE MARY. I smacked him awful hard— Shall I punish myself?

MARY. It will have to be pretty bad.

LITTLE MARY. (*Solemnly.*) Then I won't go down to breakfast with Daddy tomorrow, or the next day— O. K., Mother?

MARY. O. K. (*Little Mary walks, crestfallen, to door as Jane enters with extra cup and saucer. Little Mary sticks out her tongue.*)

LITTLE MARY. There's my tongue! So what? (*Exits skipping.*)

JANE. (*Laughing.*) She never lets anybody get the best of her, does she, Mrs. Haines?

MARY. My poor baby. She doesn't want to be a woman, Jane.

JANE. Who does?

MARY. Somehow, I've never minded it, Jane. (*Enter Mrs. Morehead. She is a bourgeois aristocrat of 55. Mary rises, kisses her.*)

MRS. MOREHEAD. Hello, child. 'Afternoon, Jane.

JANE. 'Afternoon, Mrs. Morehead. (*Exits to bedroom.*)

MARY. Mother, dear! (*She walks slowly to dressing table.*)

MRS. MOREHEAD. (*Cheerfully.*) Well, what's wrong? (*Sits.*)

MARY. (*Turning.*) How did you know something's wrong?

MRS. MOREHEAD. Your voice on the phone. Is it Stephen?

MARY. How did you know?

MRS. MOREHEAD. You sent for Mother. So it must be he. (*A pause.*)

MARY. I don't know how to begin, Mother.

MRS. MOREHEAD. (*Delighted to find that her instincts were correct.*) It's a woman! Who is she?

MARY. Her name is Crystal Allen. She—she's a salesgirl at Saks'. (*Mrs. Morehead's cheerful and practical manner discourages tears, so she begins to cream and tonic her face instead.*)

MRS. MOREHEAD. She's young and pretty, I suppose.

MARY. Well, yes. (*Defensively.*) But common.

MRS. MOREHEAD. (*Soothingly.*) Of course— Stephen told you?

MARY. No. I—I found out—this afternoon.

MRS. MOREHEAD. How far has it gone?

MARY. He's known her about three months.

MRS. MOREHEAD. Does Stephen know you know?

MARY. (*Shaking her head.*) I—I wanted to speak to you first.

24

(*The tears come anyway.*) Oh, Mother dear, what am I going to say to him?

MRS. MOREHEAD. *Nothing.*

MARY. *Nothing?*

MRS. MOREHEAD. My dear, I felt the same way twenty years ago.

MARY. Not Father?

MRS. MOREHEAD. Mary, in many ways your father was an exceptional man. (*Philosophically.*) That, unfortunately, was not one of them.

MARY. Did you say nothing?

MRS. MOREHEAD. Nothing. I had a wise mother, too. Listen, dear, this is not a new story. It comes to most wives.

MARY. But Stephen—

MRS. MOREHEAD. Stephen is a man. He's been married twelve years—

MARY. You mean, he's tired of me!

MRS. MOREHEAD. Stop crying. You'll make your nose red.

MARY. I'm not crying. (*Patting tonic on her face.*) This stuff stings.

MRS. MOREHEAD. (*Going to her.*) Stephen's tired of himself. Tired of feeling the same things in himself year after year. Time comes when every man's got to feel something new—when he's got to feel young again, just because he's growing old. Women are just the same. But when *we* get that way we change our hairdress. Or get a new cook. Or redecorate the house from stem to stern. But a man can't do over his office, or fire his secretary. Not even change the style of his hair. And the urge usually hits him hardest just when he's beginning to lose his hair. No, dear, a man has only one escape from his old self: to see a different self—in the mirror of some woman's eyes.

MARY. But, Mother—

MRS. MOREHEAD. This girl probably means no more to him than that new dress means to you.

MARY. But, Mother—

MRS. MOREHEAD. "But Mother, but Mother!" He's not giving anything to her that belongs to you, or you would have felt that yourself long ago.

MARY. (*Bewildered.*) Oh, I always thought I would. I love him so much.

MRS. MOREHEAD. And he loves you, baby. (*Drawing Mary beside her on chaise-longue.*) Now listen to me: Go away somewhere for a month or two. There's nothing like a good dose of another woman to make a man appreciate his wife. Mother knows!

MARY. But there's never been a lie between us before.

MRS. MOREHEAD. You mean, there's never been a *silence* between you before. Well, it's about time. Keeping still, when you *ache* to talk, is about the only sacrifice spoiled women like us ever have to make.

MARY. But I'd forgive him—

MRS. MOREHEAD. Forgive him? (*Impatiently.*) For what? For being a man? Accuse him, and you'll never get a chance to forgive him. He'd have to justify himself—

MARY. How can he!

MRS. MOREHEAD. (*Sighing.*) He can't and he *can*. Don't make him try. Either way you'd lose him. And remember, dear, it's being together at the *end* that really matters. (*Rising.*) One more piece of motherly advice: Don't confide in your girl friends!

MARY. I think they all know.

MRS. MOREHEAD. They think you don't? (*Mary nods.*) Leave it that way. If you let them advise you, they'll see to it, in the name of friendship, that you lose your husband and your home. I'm an old woman, dear, and I know my sex. (*Moving to door.*) I'm going right down this minute and get our tickets.

MARY. Our—tickets?

MRS. MOREHEAD. You're taking me to Bermuda, dear. My throat's been awfully bad. I haven't wanted to worry you, but my doctor says—

MARY. Oh, Mother darling! Thank you!

MRS. MOREHEAD. Don't thank me, dear. It's rather—*nice* to have you need Mother again. (*Exits. Phone rings. Mary answers it.*)

MARY. Yes?—Oh, Stephen— Yes, dear?—(*Distressed.*) Oh, Stephen! Oh, no—I'm not angry. It's—it's just that I wanted to see the play. Yes, I can get Mother to go with me. . . . Stephen, will you be very—late? (*It's a bit of a struggle, but she manages a cheerful voice.*) Oh, it's—all right. Have a good time. Of course, I know it's just business— No, dear—I won't wait up—Stephen. I love— (*A click. The other end has hung up. Jane enters. Mary turns her back. Her face would belie the calmness of her voice.*

Jane— The children and I will be having dinner alone—

CURTAIN

ACT I

SCENE 4

Two months later. A dressmaker's shop. We see 2 fitting booths, the same in appointment: triplex pier glasses, dressracks, smoking stands, 2 small chairs. They are divided by a mirrored partition. At rear of each booth, a curtain and a door, off a corridor, which leads to "the floor."

As curtain rises booth on L. is empty. Other booth is cluttered with dresses. 2 salesgirls are loading them over their arms.

1ST GIRL. (*With vivid resentment against a customer who has just departed.*) Well, now we can put them all back again. Makes you drag out everything in the damn store, and doesn't even buy a brassiere!

2ND GIRL. And that's the kind who always needs one.

1ST GIRL. This isn't her type. That isn't her type. I'd like to tell her what her type is.

2ND GIRL. I'd like to know.

1ST GIRL. It's the type that nobody gives a damn about! Gee, I'd like to work in a men's shop once. What can a man try on?

2ND GIRL. Ever see a man try on hats? What they go through, you'd think a head was something peculiar. (*Both girls exit. 1st Saleswoman enters booth on R., hereafter caller "Mary's booth."*)

1ST SALESWOMAN. Miss Myrtle, step in here a moment. (*Model, a handsome wench, in a slinky negligee, enters.*)

MODEL. Yes, Miss Shapiro.

1ST SALESWOMAN. If I've told you once, I've told you a thousand times, when you're modeling that dress, your stomach must lead. If you walk like this (*Pantomimes.*) you take away all the seduction. This is seduction! (*Shows model her rather unconvincing conception of a seductive walk.*)

27

MODEL. I'll try, Miss Shapiro. (*Tearfully.*) But if you had my appendix!

1ST SALESWOMAN. Well, Miss Myrtle, you can take your choice: You will either lose your job or lose your appendix! (*Exit model. In* R. *booth, hereafter called "Crystal's booth," enter 2nd Saleswoman.*)

2ND SALESWOMAN. (*To 1st and 2nd girls who have returned for another load of dresses.*) Quickly, please, I have a client waiting. (*2nd Girl exits with last of clothes as enter Crystal, followed by Saleswoman. 3rd Saleswoman is seen crossing corridor from* R. *to* L.)

1ST SALESWOMAN. (*Mary's Booth. Giving little white slip to Saleswoman who passes.*) Bring down Mrs. Haines' fittings. (*Exits, leaving booth empty.*)

2ND SALESWOMAN. (*Crystal's Booth.*) Will you open a charge?

CRYSTAL. (*Taking off gloves and hat.*) Please.

2ND SALESWOMAN. May I have the name?

CRYSTAL. (*Quite self-assured.*) Allen. Miss Crystal Allen. The Hotel Waverly.

2ND SALESWOMAN. May I have your other charges? Saks, Bergdorf, Cartier—?

CRYSTAL. (*Putting it on.*) Oh, I'll be opening those in the next few days—

2ND SALESWOMAN. Then may I have your bank?

CRYSTAL. I've no checking account either, at the moment. (*Enter Mary in her booth, with fitter and 1st Saleswoman, who carries her try-on gown. During following scene Mary undresses, gets into gay evening gown, fits.*)

1ST SALESWOMAN. (*To Mary, as they enter.*) Shall we show the things that came in while you were away?

MARY. Please. But I'd like to see some younger things than I usually wear.

2ND SALESWOMAN. (*In Crystal's Booth.*) I'm sorry, Miss Allen, but we must have one business reference—

CRYSTAL. I—er—am a friend of Miss Miriam Aarons. You know, the musical comedy star?

2ND SALESWOMAN. (*Coolly.*) Oh, yes, Miss Aarons. One of our new accounts. (*A pause, then decides to level, in a dramatic way.*) Miss Aarons had an *excellent* business reference.

CRYSTAL. (*Making the same decision.*) Such as Howard Fowler, the broker?

2ND SALESWOMAN. (*Brightly.*) Why, yes, I believe he is her broker!

CRYSTAL. (*Lightly, she was prepared for this.*) Well, if a broker's reference will do, it's Mr. Stephen Haines, 40 Wall Street.

2ND SALESWOMAN. (*Writing.*) That will do. (*A pause.*) Mrs. Haines is a very old client of ours.

CRYSTAL. (*Unprepared for that.*) Oh?

2ND SALESWOMAN. Will you try on now, or finish seeing the collection?

CRYSTAL. Have the models show in here. By the way, I've never met Mrs. Haines.

2ND SALESWOMAN. She's lovely.

CRYSTAL. So—I'd rather you didn't mention to her that I gave her husband as a reference. (*Beguiling.*) Do you mind?

2ND SALESWOMAN. (*With a faint smile.*) Oh, of course not, Miss Allen. (*Indulgently.*) We understand.

CRYSTAL. (*Angrily.*) Do you! What do you understand?

2ND SALESWOMAN. (*Flustered.*) I mean—

CRYSTAL. (*Very injured.*) Never mind.

2ND SALESWOMAN. Please, I hope you don't think I meant—

CRYSTAL. (*Laughing and very charming again.*) Of course not. Oh, it's dreadful, living in a strange city alone. You have to be so careful not to do anything people can misconstrue. You see, I don't know Mrs. Haines yet. So I'd hate to get off on the wrong foot before I've met her *socially*.

2ND SALESWOMAN. (*Sounds convinced.*) Naturally. Women are funny about little things like that. We never discuss one client with another. (*Mary's Booth—enter Sylvia.*)

SYLVIA. Yoo-hoo! May I come in?

MARY. (*Not at all pleased to see her.*) Hello, Sylvia.

2ND SALESWOMAN. (*In Crystal's Booth.*) What are you most interested in, Miss Allen, evening gowns?

CRYSTAL. Until I—I organize my social life—I won't have much use for evening gowns.

2ND SALESWOMAN. I'll show you some smart daytime things. (*Deliberately toneless.*) And we have very exciting negligees— (*They exit. Mary's Booth: Sylvia circles around Mary, appraising her fitting with a critical eye.*)

MARY. Oh, sit down, Sylvia.

SYLVIA. (*To the Fitter.*) I don't like that underslung line. (*Demonstrating on Mary.*) It cuts her across the fanny. Makes her look positively duck-bottomed.

MARY. (*Pulling away.*) It's so tight, Mrs. Fowler can't sit down.

1ST SALESWOMAN. Mrs. Fowler, shall I see if your fittings are ready?

SYLVIA. They'll call me.

MARY. (*Pointing to dress 1st Saleswoman has over her arm.*) Have you seen that?

1ST SALESWOMAN. (*Holding up dress.*) It's a lovely shape on. It doesn't look like a thing in the hand. (*Hands dress to someone outside and calls.*) Tell Princess Tamara to show this model.

SYLVIA. (*Settling in chair and smoking cigarette.*) So you had a marvelous time in Bermuda.

MARY. I had a good rest.

SYLVIA. (*With unconscious humor.*) Howard wants *me* to take a world cruise. By the way, dear, how is Stephen?

MARY. Splendid. (*Smiling, and very glad to be able to tell Sylvia this.*) He's not nearly so busy. He hasn't spent an evening—in the office, since I've come home. (*Enter 1st model in an elaborate negligee. Mary shakes her head, very practical.*) Pretty, but I never need a thing like that—

SYLVIA. Of course *you* don't. A hot little number, for intimate afternoons. (*Exit 1st model.*) Howard says nobody's seen Stephen in the Club, in the afternoon, for months—

MARY. (*Thought flashes across her mind that Stephen could, of course, have revised his extra-marital schedule, from an evening to an afternoon one, but she quickly dismisses it. Stephen has never let anything interfere with his hours downtown.*) Don't worry so much about Stephen, Sylvia. He's my concern. (*Enter 2nd Model in a corset. She is prettily fashioned from head to toe. She does a great deal for the wisp of lace she wears. It does nothing that nature didn't do better for her.*)

2ND MODEL. This is our new one-piece lace foundation garment. (*Pirouettes.*) Zips up the back, and no bones. (*She exits.*)

SYLVIA. Just that uplift, Mary, you need. I always said you'd regret nursing. Look at me. I don't think there's another girl our age who can boast of bazooms like mine. I've taken care of them. Ice water every morning, camphor at night.

30

MARY. Doesn't it smell rather like an old fur coat? (*Princess Tamara passes in corridor.*)

SYLVIA. Who cares?

MARY. Well, doesn't Howard?

SYLVIA. (*Laughing harshly.*) Howard! With his prostate condition?

1ST SALESWOMAN. (*Calling out door.*) Princess Tamara, show in here. (*Enter Princess Tamara in a very extreme evening gown. She is Russian, regal, soignée.*)

MARY. Oh, Tamara, how lovely!

TAMARA. You must have it. Stephen would be amazed.

MARY. He certainly would. It's too extreme for me.

SYLVIA. (*Rises.*) And you really haven't the figure. (*Yanks at gown.*) Tamara, you wear it wrong. I saw it in *Vogue*. (*Jerks.*) Up here, and down there.

TAMARA. (*Slapping Sylvia's hand down.*) Stop mauling me!

1ST SALESWOMAN. Princess!

TAMARA. What do you know how to wear clothes?

SYLVIA. I am not a model, Tamara, but no one disputes how I wear clothes!

TAMARA. No one has mistaken you for the Duchess of Windsor yet?

1ST SALESWOMAN. Princess Tamara, please apologize.

MARY. (*To Saleswoman.*) It's just professional jealousy. They both wear clothes so beautifully. They're really friends!

SYLVIA. (*Maliciously.*) You mean Tamara and *Howard* are friends.

TAMARA. (*Disgusted at the thought.*) Do you accuse me of flirting with your husband?

SYLVIA. (*Pleasantly.*) Go as far as you can, Tamara! If I know Howard, you're wasting valuable time.

TAMARA. (*Very angry.*) Perhaps I am. But perhaps somebody else is not! (*Saleswoman gives her an angry shove.*) You are riding for a fall-off, Sylvia dear! (*Exit Tamara angrily, followed by Saleswoman.*)

SYLVIA. Did you get that inyouendo? I'd like to see Howard Fowler put anything over on me. Oh, I've always hated that girl, exploiting her title the way she does! (*Crystal and 2nd Saleswoman enter Crystal's Booth.*)

2ND SALESWOMAN. (*Calling down corridor.*) Princess Tamara,

show in here, to Miss Allen. (*Mary's Saleswoman enters Mary's Booth, picking up the call.*)

1ST SALESWOMAN. Girls, show in Number 3 to Miss Allen.

SYLVIA. (*Alert.*) Did you say Miss Allen?

1ST SALESWOMAN. Yes.

SYLVIA. Not—Crystal Allen?

1ST SALESWOMAN. Why, yes—I just saw her on the floor. She's so attractive I asked her name.

SYLVIA. (*Watching Mary closely.*) Oh, so Crystal Allen gets her things here now? (*Mary sits down suddenly.*)

1ST SALESWOMAN. She's a new client— Why, Mrs. Haines, are you ill? (*Mary has caught Sylvia's eye in the mirror. Sylvia knows now that Mary knows.*)

MARY. No, no. I'm just tired. (*Tamara enters Crystal's Booth.*)

FITTER. We've kept you standing too long—

1ST SALESWOMAN. I'll get you a glass of sherry. (*Exit Mary's fitter and Saleswoman. Sylvia closes door.*)

CRYSTAL. (*Crystal's Booth. Admiring Tamara's extreme evening gown.*) I'm going to have that, if I have to wear it for breakfast.

2ND SALESWOMAN. Send it in here, Princess. (*Tamara exits.*)

SYLVIA. (*Mary's Booth.*) Mary, you do know! (*Deeply sympathetic.*) Why didn't you confide in me?

MARY. Sylvia, go away.

SYLVIA. (*Fiercely.*) Stephen is a louse. Spending your money on a girl like that.

MARY. Sylvia, please mind your own affairs.

SYLVIA. She's already made a fool of you before all your friends. And don't you think the salesgirls know who gets the bills?

MARY. (*Distraught.*) I don't care, I tell you. I don't care!

SYLVIA. Oh, yes, you do. (*Pointing to Mary's stricken face in mirror.*) Don't be an ostrich, Mary. (*A pause.*) Go in there and face her down.

MARY. I'm going home. (*She rises and begins to dress.*)

1ST SALESWOMAN. (*Half enters.*) Mrs. Haines' sherry—

SYLVIA. (*Taking it from her, and closing door in her face.*) All right. You've caught her cold. It's your chance to humiliate her. Just say a few quiet words. Tell her you'll make Stephen's life hell until he gives her up.

MARY. Stephen will give her up when he's tired of her.

SYLVIA. When he's tired of her? Look where she was six months ago. Look where she is now. She probably has an apartment to go with those kinds of clothes.

MARY. Stephen's not in love with that girl.

SYLVIA. Maybe not. But you don't know women like that when they get hold of a man.

MARY. Sylvia, please let me decide what is best for me, and my home. (*Crystal, in her booth, has been undressing, admiring herself as she does so in mirror. Now she slips into a "really exciting" negligee. During the scene going on in Mary's Booth she tries to get out of the negligee easily. She can't.*)

SYLVIA. Well, she may be a perfectly marvelous influence for Stephen, but she's not going to do your children any good.

MARY. (*Turning to her.*) What do you mean?

SYLVIA. (*Mysteriously.*) Never mind.

MARY. (*Going to her.*) Tell me!

SYLVIA. Far be it from *me* to tell you things you don't care to hear. I've known this all along. (*Nobly.*) Have I uttered?

MARY. (*Violently.*) What have my children to do with this?

SYLVIA. (*After all, Mary's asking for it.*) It was while you were away. Edith saw them. Stephen, and that tramp, and your children—together, lunching in the Park.

MARY. It's not true!

SYLVIA. Why would Edith lie? She said they were having a hilarious time. Little Stevie was eating his lunch sitting on that woman's lap. She was kissing him between every bite. When I heard that, I was positively heart-sick, dear! (*Sees she has scored. Celebrates by tossing down Mary's sherry.*)

CRYSTAL. (*Crystal's Booth.*) Oh, go get that evening gown. This thing is too complicated to get out of.

2ND SALESWOMAN. Right away, Miss Allen. (*Exits.*)

SYLVIA. (*Mary's Booth.*) But, as you say, dear, it's your affair, not mine. (*Goes to door, looking very hurt that Mary has refused her good advice.*) No doubt that girl will make a perfectly good stepmamma for your children! (*Exits. Mary, now dressed, is alone. She stares at partition which separates her from that still unmeasured enemy to her well-ordered domesticity, "the other woman." Her common sense dictates she should go home, but now she violently experiences the ache to talk. She struggles against it, then goes, bitterly determined, to door. Exits. A second later, a knock on Crystal's door. Crystal is alone.*)

33

CRYSTAL. Come in! (*Enter Mary. She closes door.*) I beg your pardon?

MARY. I am—Mrs. Stephen Haines.

CRYSTAL. (*Her poise is admirable.*) Sorry—I don't think I know you!

MARY. Please don't pretend.

CRYSTAL. So Stephen finally told you?

MARY. No. I found out. (*2nd Saleswoman half enters.*)

CRYSTAL. Stay out of here! (*Exit Saleswoman.*)

MARY. I've known about you from the beginning.

CRYSTAL. Well, that is news.

MARY. I've kept still up to now—

CRYSTAL. Very smart of you. (*2nd Saleswoman pantomimes down corridor to another girl to join her. Enters Mary's booth. One by one, during rest of this scene, Fitter, Saleswoman, and models tiptoe into Mary's booth and plaster their ears against partition.*)

MARY. But you've gone a little too far— You've been seeing my children. I won't have you touching my children!

CRYSTAL. Fod God's sake, don't get hysterical. What do I care about your children? I'm sick of hearing about them.

MARY. You won't have to hear about them any more. When Stephen realizes how humiliating all this has been to me, he'll give you up instantly.

CRYSTAL. Says who? The dog in the manger?

MARY. That's all I have to say. (*Turns to go.*)

CRYSTAL. That's plenty. Maybe you'll find you've said too much. Stephen's not tired of me yet, Mrs. Haines.

MARY. (*Contemptuous.*) Stephen is just amusing himself with you.

CRYSTAL. And he's amusing himself plenty.

MARY. You're very hard.

CRYSTAL. I can be soft—on the *right* occasions. What do you expect me to do? Burst into tears and beg you to forgive me?

MARY. I found exactly what I expected!

CRYSTAL. That goes double!

MARY. (*Turning to door.*) You'll have to make other plans, Miss Allen.

CRYSTAL. (*Going to her.*) Listen, I'm taking my marching orders from Stephen.

MARY. Stephen doesn't love you.

34

CRYSTAL. He's doing the best he can in the circumstances.

MARY. He couldn't love a girl like you.

CRYSTAL. What do you think we've been doing for the past six months? Crossword puzzles? What have you got to kick about? You've got everything that matters. The name, the position, the money—

MARY. (*Losing control of herself again.*) Nothing matters to me but Stephen—!

CRYSTAL. Oh, can the sob-stuff, Mrs. Haines. You don't think this is the first time Stephen's ever cheated? Listen, I'd break up your smug little roost if I could. I have just as much right as you have to sit in a tub of butter. But I don't stand a chance!

MARY. I'm glad you know it.

CRYSTAL. Well, don't think it's just because he's *fond* of you—

MARY. *Fond?*

CRYSTAL. You're not what's stopping him— You're just an old *habit* with him. It's just those brats he's afraid of losing. If he weren't such a sentimental fool about those kids, he'd have walked out on *you* months ago.

MARY. (*Fiercely.*) That's not true!

CRYSTAL. Oh, yes, it is. I'm telling you a few plain truths you won't get from Stephen.

MARY. Stephen's always told me the truth—!

CRYSTAL. (*Maliciously.*) Well, look at the record. (*A pause.*) Listen, Stephen's satisfied with this arrangement. So don't force any issue, unless you want plenty of trouble.

MARY. You've made it impossible for me to do anything else—!

CRYSTAL. (*Rather pleased.*) Have I?

MARY. You haven't played fair—!

CRYSTAL. Where would any of us get if we played fair?

MARY. Where do you hope to get?

CRYSTAL. Right where *you* are, Mrs. Haines!

MARY. You're very confident.

CRYSTAL. The longer you stay in here, the more confident I get. Saint or no saint, Mrs. Haines, you are a hell of a stupid *woman!*

MARY. (*Mary stares at her wide-eyed at the horrid thought that this may be the truth. She refuses to meet the challenge. She equivocates.*) I probably am. I— (*Suddenly ashamed that she has allowed herself to be put so pathetically on the defensive.*) Oh, why am I standing here talking to you? This is something for Stephen and me to settle! (*Exits.*)

CRYSTAL. (*Slamming door after her.*) Oh, what the hell!

2ND SALESWOMAN. (*Mary's Booth.*) So that's what she calls meeting Mrs. Haines *socially.*

1ST SALESWOMAN. Gee, I feel sorry for Mrs. Haines. She's so nice.

NEGLIGEE MODEL. She should have kept her mouth shut. Now she's in the soup.

1ST SALESWOMAN. It's a terrible mistake to force a decision on a man who's hot for another woman.

1ST MODEL. Allen's smart. She knows that.

1ST SALESWOMAN. She'll get him sure.

1ST FITTER. Look at that body. She's got him now.

2ND SALESWOMAN. You can't trust any man. *That's* all they want.

CORSET MODEL. (*Plaintively, her hands on her lovely hips.*) What else have we got to give?

CURTAIN

ACT I

Scene 5

2 *weeks later. Small exercise room in Elizabeth Arden's beauty-salon.* R., *a mirrored wall. Rear, a door.* L., *cabinet victrola beneath open window. On floor, a wadded pink satin mat. As curtain rises, Sylvia, in a pair of shorts, is prone on mat, describing lackadaisical arcs with her legs, to the sensuous rhythm of a tango record. Instructress, a bright, pretty girl in a pink silk bathing suit, stands above her, drilling her in a carefully cultured voice. Until the cue "stretch," Instructress' lines are spoken through Sylvia's prattle, which she is determined, for the honor of the salon, to ignore, and, if possible, to discourage. From word "up," this is a hopeless task.*

INSTRUCTRESS. Up—over—up—down. Up—stretch—up—together. Up—stretch—up—

SYLVIA. Of course, my sympathies are for Mrs. Haines. They always are for a woman against a man—

INSTRUCTRESS. (*Louder.*) Up—over—up—down. Up—stretch —up—together. Up—

SYLVIA. But she did behave like an awful idiot—

INSTRUCTRESS. Stretch—up—together. Please don't try to talk, Mrs. Fowler.

SYLVIA. But you know how some women are when they lose their heads—

INSTRUCTRESS. (*Grimly.*) Stretch—up—together—up—

SYLVIA. They do things they regret all their lives—

INSTRUCTRESS. (*Grabs Sylvia's languid limb and gives it a corrective yank.*) Ster-retch!

SYLVIA. Ouch, my scars!

INSTRUCTRESS. (*Callously.*) This is very good for adhesions. Up—

SYLVIA. (*Resolutely inert.*) It's got me down.

INSTRUCTRESS. Rest. (*Sylvia groans her relief.*) And relax your diaphragm muscles, Mrs. Fowler, (*Bitterly.*) if you can. (*Goes to victrola, changes record for a fox-trot.*)

SYLVIA. Of course, I do wish Mrs. Haines would make up her mind if she's going to get a divorce. It's terrible on all her friends, not knowing. Naturally, you can't ask them anywhere—

INSTRUCTRESS. Of course not. Now, on your side. (*Sylvia rolls to her side, reclining on her elbow.*) Ready? Up—down—up— down— (*Snaps her fingers. Sylvia flaps a limp leg up, down.*) Don't bend the knee—

SYLVIA. (*Thoughtfully.*) Of course, for the children's sake, I think Mrs. Haines ought to stay. (*Piously.*) I know I would. (*Her knees look bent, not to say broken.*)

INSTRUCTRESS. (*Imploring.*) Don't crook it, please.

SYLVIA. And she ought not to have faced Mr. Haines with the issue. When a man's got himself in that deep he has to have time to taper it off—

INSTRUCTRESS. (*Straightening out Sylvia's offending member with considerable force.*) Thigh in, not out.

SYLVIA. (*Pained, but undaunted.*) But Mrs. Haines never listens to any of her friends. She is a very peculiar woman.

INSTRUCTRESS. She must be. Now, please—up—down—up— down—

SYLVIA. (*Redoubling her efforts, and her errors.*) Oh, I tell everybody whatever she wants to do is the right thing. I've got to be loyal to Mrs. Haines, you know. . . . Oh, I'm simply exhausted. (*Flops over, flat on her stomach, panting.*)

INSTRUCTRESS. Then suppose you try something simple—like crawling up the wall? (*Sylvia lifts a martyred face. Instructress changes record for a waltz.*)

SYLVIA. (*Scrambling to her feet.*) What I go through to keep my figure! Lord, it infuriates me at dinner parties when some fat lazy man asks, "What do you do with yourself all day, Mrs. Fowler?" (*Sits alongside the rear wall.*)

INSTRUCTRESS. You rotate on your buttocks. (*Sylvia rotates, then lies back, her knees drawn up to her chin, the soles of her feet against wall.*) Arms flat. Now you crawl slowly up the wall.

SYLVIA. (*Crawling.*) I wish you wouldn't say that. It makes me feel like vermin—

INSTRUCTRESS. (*Kneeling beside her.*) Don't talk.

SYLVIA. There's a couple of people I'd like to exterminate, too—

INSTRUCTRESS. Let's reverse the action. (*Sylvia crawls down, as Peggy enters in exercise suit. Instructress brightens.*) How do you do, Mrs. Day? (*To Sylvia.*) Down slowly—

PEGGY. (*Gaily.*) How do you do? Hello, Sylvia.

SYLVIA. You're late again, Peggy.

PEGGY. (*Crestfallen.*) I'm sorry.

SYLVIA. (*Sitting up.*) After all, dear, I am paying for this course.

PEGGY. You know I'm grateful, Sylvia—

SYLVIA. Well, don't cry about it. It's only fifty dollars.

PEGGY. That's a lot to me—

SYLVIA. (*Sweetly.*) To you, or just to your husband, dear?

INSTRUCTRESS. Please, ladies. Let us begin with posture. (*Sylvia rises.*) A lady always enters a room erect.

SYLVIA. Lots of my friends exit horizontally. (*Peggy and Sylvia go to mirrored wall, stand with backs to it.*)

INSTRUCTRESS. Now—knees apart. Sit on the wall. (*They sit on imaginary seats.*) Relax. (*They bend forward from waist, finger tips brushing floor.*) Now, roll slowly up the wall . . . pressing each little vertebra against the wall as hard as you can . . . shoulders back, and where they belong. Heads back. Mrs. Fowler, lift yourself behind the ears. Pretend you're just a silly little puppet dangling on a string. Chin up. (*She places her hand at level of*

Peggy's straining chin.) No, Mrs. Day, your chin is resting comfortably on a little table. Elbows bent—up on your toes—arms out —shove with the small of your back—you're off! (*Sylvia and Peggy, side by side, mince across room.*)

PEGGY. (*Whispering.*) Oh, Sylvia, why do you always insinuate that John is practically a—miser?

INSTRUCTRESS. (*She refers to Peggy's swaying hips.*) Tuck under!

SYLVIA. You have your own little income, Peggy. And what do you do with it? You give it to John—

INSTRUCTRESS. Now, back, please! (*They mince backwards across room.*)

PEGGY. (*Staunchly.*) John makes so little—

INSTRUCTRESS. (*She refers to Sylvia's relaxed tummy*) Steady center control!

SYLVIA. Peggy, you're robbing John of his manly sense of responsibility. You're turning him into a gigolo. A little money of her own she lets no man touch is the only protection a woman has. (*They are against mirror again.*)

INSTRUCTRESS. Now, are you both the way you were when you left the wall?

SYLVIA. (*Brightly.*) Well, I am.

INSTRUCTRESS. No, Mrs. Fowler, you're not. (*She imitates Sylvia's posture, showing how Sylvia's posterior protrudes, against the dictates of fashion, if not of nature.*) Not this, Mrs. Fowler— ("Bumps.") That! (*She leads Sylvia forward.*) Try it, please. (*Facing one another, they do an elegant pair of "bumps."*) Now, relax on the mat. (*This piece of business defies description, but to do the best one can: Girls stand side by side, arms straight above their heads. At Instructress' count of "one," each drops a hand, limp, from wrist. At "two," the other hand drops, then their heads fall upon their breasts, their arms flap to their sides, their waists cave in, their knees buckle under, and they swoon, or crumble like boneless things, to the mat. Instructress has changed record.*) Now, ready? Bend—stretch, you know. Begin— (*They do another leg exercise on mat.*) Bend—stretch—bend—down— plenty of pull on the hamstrings, please! Bend—stretch—bend— down— (*Enter Edith. She is draped in a white sheet. Her head is bound in a white towel. Her face is undergoing a "tie-up," that is, she wears broad white straps under her chin and across her forehead. She appears very distressed.*)

EDITH. Oh, Sylvia! Hello, Peggy—

SYLVIA. (*Sitting up.*) Why, Edith, what are you doing up here?

EDITH. Having a facial, downstairs. Oh, Sylvia, I'm so glad you're here. I've done the most *awful* thing. I—

INSTRUCTRESS. We're right in the middle of our exercise, Mrs. Potter—

SYLVIA. (*To Instructress.*) Will you tell them outside—I want my parafine bath now? There's a dear.

INSTRUCTRESS. But, Mrs. Fowler—

SYLVIA. (*Cajoling.*) I'm simply exhausted.

INSTRUCTRESS. You've hardly moved a muscle.

SYLVIA. (*With elaborate patience.*) Look, whose carcass is this? Yours or mine?

INSTRUCTRESS. It's yours, Mrs. Fowler, but I'm paid to exercise it.

SYLVIA. You talk like a horse-trainer.

INSTRUCTRESS. Well, Mrs. Fowler, you're getting warm. (*Exits.*)

EDITH. I've done the most *ghastly* thing. Move over. (*Peggy and Sylvia move over, Edith plumps between them on mat.*) But it wasn't until I got here, in the middle of my facial, that I realized it—I could bite my tongue off when I think of it—

SYLVIA. Well, what is it, Edith?

EDITH. I was lunching with Frances Jones, and—

SYLVIA. Edith Potter, I know exactly what you're going to say!

EDITH. I forgot she—

SYLVIA. You forgot she's Dolly de Peyster.

EDITH. But I never read her awful column—

SYLVIA. (*Fiercely.*) You told her something about me? What did you tell her?

EDITH. Oh, darling, you know I never give you away. (*Remorsefully.*) I—I—told her all about Stephen and Mary—

SYLVIA. (*Relieved.*) Oh! That!

EDITH. It wasn't until the middle of my facial—

PEGGY. Oh, Edith! It will be in all those dreadful tabloids!

EDITH. I know—I've been racking my brains to recall what I said— I think I told her that when Mary walked into the fitting room, she yanked the ermine coat off the Allen girl—

SYLVIA. You didn't!

EDITH. Well, I don't know whether I said ermine or *sable*—but I know I told her that Mary *smacked* the Allen girl!

PEGGY. Edith!

EDITH. Well, that's what Sylvia told me!

SYLVIA. I didn't!

EDITH. You did, too!

SYLVIA. (*Hurt.*) Anyway, I didn't expect you to tell it to a cheap reporter—

EDITH. Well, it doesn't really make much difference. The divorce is practically settled—

SYLVIA. (*Eagerly.*) Who says so?

EDITH. You did!

SYLVIA. (*Patiently.*) I said, Mary couldn't broadcast her domestic difficulties, and not expect them to wind up in a scandal.

PEGGY. Mary didn't broadcast them!

SYLVIA. Who did?

PEGGY. *You* did. You—you're all making it impossible for her to do anything now but get a divorce!

SYLVIA. You flatter us. We didn't realize how much influence we had on our friends' lives!

PEGGY. Everybody calling her up, telling her how badly she's been treated—

SYLVIA. As a matter of fact, I told her she'd make a great mistake. What has any woman got to gain by a divorce? No matter how much he gives her, she won't have what they have together. And you know as well as I do, he'd marry that girl. What he's spent on her, he'd have to, to protect his investment. (*Sorrowfully.*) But I have as much influence on Mary as I have on *you*, Peggy. (*Instructress re-enters.*)

INSTRUCTRESS. The paraffine bath is ready, Mrs. Fowler.

SYLVIA. (*Rises.*) Well, don't worry, Edith, I'll give de Peyster a ring. I can fix it.

EDITH. How?

SYLVIA. (*Graciously.*) Oh, I'll tell her you were lying.

EDITH. You'll do no such thing!

SYLVIA. (*Shrugging.*) Then let the story ride. It will be forgotten tomorrow. You know the awful things they printed about—what's her name?—before she jumped out the window? Why, I can't even remember her name, so who cares, Edith? (*Exits.*)

INSTRUCTRESS. Mrs. Potter, you come right back where you belong.

EDITH. Why, you'd think this was a boarding school!

INSTRUCTRESS. But, Mrs. Potter, it's such a foolish waste of money—

EDITH. Listen, relaxing is part of my facial.

INSTRUCTRESS. (*Coolly.*) Then you should relax completely, Mrs. Potter, from the chin up. (*Exits.*)

EDITH. Honestly, the class feeling you run into these days! (*Struggles to her feet.*) I'm so tired of paying creatures like that to insult me—

PEGGY. (*Going to her.*) Edith! Let's call Mary up and warn her!

EDITH. About what?

PEGGY. The newspapers!

EDITH. My dear, how could we do that, without involving Sylvia—

PEGGY. But it's her fault— Oh, she's such a dreadful woman!

EDITH. Oh, she can't help it, Peggy. It's just her tough luck she wasn't born deaf and dumb. But what can we do about it? She's always gotten away with murder. Why, she's been having an affair for a year with that young customers' man in Howard's office.

PEGGY. (*Shocked.*) Edith!

EDITH. Right under Howard's nose! But Howard doesn't care! So what business is it of yours or mine? (*Earnestly.*) Peggy, take a tip from me—keep out of other women's troubles. I've never had a fight with a girl friend in all my life. Why? I hear no evil, I see no evil, I speak no evil!

CURTAIN

ACT I

SCENE 6

A few days later.
Mary's pantry, midnight. L., a swinging door to kitchen. Rear, a sink under curtained window. A small, built-in refrigerator. C., a table, 2 chairs.
As curtain rises, Jane, the maid, and Maggie, the new

cook, are having a midnight snack. Maggie, a buxom, middle-aged woman, wears wrapper and felt bedroom slippers.

JANE. (*Folding tabloid newspaper she has been reading to Maggie.*) So he says, "All you can do with a story like that is live it down, Mary."

MAGGIE. I told you they'd begin all over. Once a thing like that is out between a married couple, they've got to fight it out. Depends which they get sick of first, each other, or the argument.

JANE. It's enough to make you lose your faith in marriage.

MAGGIE. Whose faith in marriage?

JANE. You don't believe in marriage?

MAGGIE. Sure I do. For women. (*Sighs.*) But it's the sons of Adam they got to marry. Go on.

JANE. Well, finally he said to the madam, "I gave her up, didn't I? And I was a swine, about the way I did it." How do you suppose he did it, Maggie?

MAGGIE. Maybe he just said, "Scram, the wife is onto us."

JANE. Well, the madam didn't believe him. She says, "Stephen, you really ain't seen her?"

MAGGIE. He lied in his teeth—

JANE. Oh, the way he said it, I kind of believed him. But the madam says, "Oh, but can I ever trust you again?"

MAGGIE. You can't trust none of 'em no further than I can kick this lemon pie.

JANE. Oh, it was terrible sad. He said, "Mary, dear Mary, Mary, dear Mary, Mary—"

MAGGIE. Dear Mary. But it ain't exactly convincing.

JANE. Then, I guess he tried to kiss her. Because she says, "Please don't. I'll never be able to kiss you again without thinking of her in your arms."

MAGGIE. (*Appreciatively.*) Just like in the movies— Imagine him taking up with a girl like that.

JANE. He was telling the madam: She's a virgin.

MAGGIE. She *is*? Then what's all the rumpus about?

JANE. Oh, she ain't a virgin now. She was.

MAGGIE. So was Mae West—once.

JANE. He told the madam he'd been faithful for twelve years.

MAGGIE. Well, that's something these days; that beats Lind-

43

bergh's flight. Did the madam believe him?

JANE. She said, "How do I know you've been faithful?"

MAGGIE. She don't.

JANE. But the way he said it—

MAGGIE. Listen, if they lay off six months, they feel themselves busting out all over with haloes.

JANE. Anyway, he says this girl was really a nice girl. So sweet and interested in him and all. And how it happened one night, unexpected, in her room—

MAGGIE. Did he think it was going to happen in Roxy's?

JANE. He said she wouldn't take nothing from him for months—

MAGGIE. Only her education. Oh, that one knew her onions. She certainly played him for a sucker.

JANE. That's what the madam said. She said, "Stephen, can't you see that girl's only interested in you for your money?"

MAGGIE. Tch, tch, tch. I'll bet that made him sore. A man don't like to be told no woman but his wife is fool enough to love him. It drives 'em nutty.

JANE. Did it! "Mary, I told you what kind of girl she is," he says. You know—I just told you—

MAGGIE. I had her number. You didn't convey no information.

JANE. Well, then they both got sore.

MAGGIE. (Rises, goes out for coffee.) I knew it.

JANE. So he began to tell her all over what a good husband he'd been. And how hard he'd worked for her and the kids. And she kept interrupting with what a good wife she'd been and how proud she was of him. Then they began to exaggerate themselves—

MAGGIE. (Enters with coffeepot.) Listen, anybody that's ever been married knows that line backwards and forwards. What happened?

JANE. Well, somewhere in there the madam says, "Stephen, you do want a divorce. Only you ain't got the courage to ask it." And he says, "Oh, my God, no, I don't, Mary. Haven't I told you?" And she says, "But you don't love me!" And he says, "But oh, my God, Mary, I'm awful fond of you." And she says, very icy, "Fond, fond? Is that all?" and he says, "No, Mary, there's the children." Maggie, that's the thing I don't understand. Why does she get so mad every time he says they've got to consider the children? If children ain't the point of being married, what is?

MAGGIE. A woman don't want to be told she's being kept on just to run a kindergarten. (*Goes to icebox for bottle of cream.*)

JANE. Well, the madam says, "Stephen, I want to keep the children out of this. I haven't used the children. I ain't asked you to sacrifice yourself for the children." Maggie, that's where he got so terrible mad. He says, "But why, in God's name, Mary? You knew about us all along. Why did you wait until now to make a fool of me?"

MAGGIE. As if he needed her help.

JANE. So then, suddenly she says, in a awful low voice, "Stephen, oh, Stephen, we can't go on like this. It ain't worthy of what we been to each other!" And he says, "Oh, no, it's not, Mary!"

MAGGIE. Quite a actress, ain't you?

JANE. My boy friend says I got eyes like Joan Crawford.

MAGGIE. Did he ever say anything about your legs? Have a cup of coffee. (*Pours coffee.*)

JANE. That's when the madam says what you could have knocked me down with a feather! The madam says, "Stephen, I want a divorce. Yes, Stephen, *I* want a divorce!"

MAGGIE. Tch. Tch. Abdicating!

JANE. Well, Maggie, you could have knocked him down with a feather!

MAGGIE. (*Waving coffeepot.*) I'd like to knock him down with this.

JANE. "My God! Mary," he says, "you don't mean it!" So she says, in a funny voice, "Yes, I do. You've killed my love for you, Stephen."

MAGGIE. He's just simple-minded enough to believe that.

JANE. So he says, "I don't blame you. My God, how can I blame you?"

MAGGIE. My God, he can't!

JANE. So then she said it was all over, because it was only the children he minded losing. She said that made their marriage a mockery.

MAGGIE. A mockery?

JANE. Something funny.

MAGGIE. I ain't going to die laughing.

JANE. He said she was talking nonsense. He said she was just upset on account of this story in the papers. He said what else could she expect if she was going to spill her troubles to a lot of gabby women? He said she should go to bed until she could think things over. He was going out for a breath of fresh air.

MAGGIE. The old hat trick.

JANE. So the madam says, "You're going to see that girl." And he says, "Oh, for God's sake, Mary, one minute you never want to see me again, the next I can't even go out for a airing!"

MAGGIE. You oughtn't to let none of 'em out except on a leash.

JANE. And she says, "Are you going to see her, or ain't you?" And he says, "Well, what difference does it make, if you're going to divorce me?" And she says, "It don't make no difference to *you*, I guess. Please go, Stephen. And don't come back *ever*." (*Begins to cry*.)

MAGGIE. (*Impatiently*.) Yes?

JANE. I didn't hear his last words. Because naturally, when he said he was going, I scooted down the hall. But I heard her call, "Stephen?" and he stops on the landing and says, "Yes, Mary?" and she says, "Nothing. Just don't slam the front door—the servants will hear you!" So I came down here. Oh, Maggie, what's going to happen?

MAGGIE. She's going to get a divorce.

JANE. Oh, dear. I'm so sad for her.

MAGGIE. I ain't.

JANE. What?

MAGGIE. She's indulging a pride she ain't entitled to. Marriage is a business of taking care of a man and rearing his children. It ain't meant to be no perpetual honeymoon. How long would any husband last if he was supposed to go on acting forever like a red-hot Clark Gable? What's the difference if he don't love her?

JANE. How can you say that, Maggie!

MAGGIE. That don't let her off her obligation to keep him from making a fool of himself, does it?

JANE. Do you think he'll marry that girl?

MAGGIE. When a man's got the habit of supporting some woman, he just don't feel natural unless he's doing it.

JANE. But he told the madam marrying her was the furthest thing from his mind.

MAGGIE. It don't matter what he's got in his mind. It's what those two women got in theirs will settle the matter.

JANE. But the madam says it's up to *him*. She said, "You love her, or you love me, Stephen."

MAGGIE. So what did he say to that?

JANE. Nothing for a long time. Just walked up and down—up and down—up and—

MAGGIE. He was thinking. Tch—tch. The first man who can think up a good explanation how he can be in love with his wife *and* another woman is going to win that prize they're always giving out in Sweden!

CURTAIN

ACT I

Scene 7

A month later. Mary's living room. The room is now denuded of pictures, books, vases, etc. Rug is rolled up. Curtains and chairs covered with slips.

As curtain rises, Mary, dressed for traveling, is pacing up and down. Mrs. Morehead, dressed for the street, watches her from sofa.

MRS. MOREHEAD. What time does your train go?

MARY. (*Looking at her wrist watch.*) An hour. His secretary ought to be here. I never knew there could be so many papers to sign.

MRS. MOREHEAD. You showed everything to your lawyers—

MARY. They always say the same thing! I'm getting a "raw deal"—

MRS. MOREHEAD. (*Alarmed.*) But, Mary—

MARY. Oh, I know it's not true. Stephen's been very generous.

MRS. MOREHEAD. Oh, I wouldn't say that. If Stephen is a rich man now, he owes it largely to you.

MARY. Stephen would have gotten where he is with or without me.

MRS. MOREHEAD. He didn't have a penny when you married him.

MARY. Mother, are you trying to make me bitter, too?

MRS. MOREHEAD. (*Helplessly.*) I'm sure I don't know what to say. If I sympathize with Stephen, you accuse me of taking his

47

side. And when I sympathize with you, I'm making you bitter. The thing for me to do is keep still. (*Pause. Then, emphatically.*) You're both making a terrible mistake!

MARY. Mother, please!

MRS. MOREHEAD. But the children, Mary. The children—

MARY. What good will it do them to be brought up in a home full of quarrelling and suspicion? They'll be better off just with me.

MRS. MOREHEAD. No, they won't. A child needs both its parents in one home.

MARY. A home without love?

MRS. MOREHEAD. He's terribly fond of you—

MARY. Mother, don't use that word! Oh, Mother, please. Every argument goes round in circles. And it's too late now—

MRS. MOREHEAD. It's never too late when you love. Mary, why don't you call this thing off? I'm sure that's what Stephen's waiting for.

MARY. (*Bitterly.*) Is it? He hasn't made any sign of it to me. Isn't he the one to come to me?

MRS. MOREHEAD. You're the one, Mary, who insisted on the divorce.

MARY. But don't you see, if he hadn't wanted it, he'd have fought me—

MRS. MOREHEAD. Stephen's not the fighting kind.

MARY. Neither am I.

MRS. MOREHEAD. Damn these modern laws!

MARY. Mother!

MRS. MOREHEAD. Damn them, I say! Fifty years ago, when women couldn't get divorces, they made the best of situations like this. And sometimes, out of situations like this, they made very good things indeed! (*Enter Jane, R.*)

JANE. Mr. Haines' secretary, ma'am.

MRS. MOREHEAD. Tell her to come in. (*Exit Jane.*) Now, go bathe your eyes. Don't let that adding-machine see you like this. And don't be long. Remember, you have one more unpleasant task.

MARY. Mary?

MRS. MOREHEAD. The child must be told.

MARY. (*Miserably, a little guiltily.*) I have been putting it off. Because—

MRS. MOREHEAD. Because you hope at the last minute a miracle

will keep you from making a mess of your life. Have you thought:
Stephen might marry that girl?

MARY. (*Very confident.*) He won't do that.

MRS. MOREHEAD. What makes you so sure?

MARY. Because, deep down, Stephen does love me— But he won't
find it out until I've—really gone away— (*At door.*) You'll take
good care of the children, Mother? And make them write to me to
Reno once a week? And please, Mother, don't spoil them so. (*Exits*
L.)

MRS. MOREHEAD. Gracious! You'd think I'd never raised children of my own! (*Enter Miss Watts and Miss Trimmerback,* R.
*They are very tailored, plain girls. Miss Watts, the older and
plainer, carries brief-case.*) How do you do, Miss Watts?

MISS WATTS. How do you do, Mrs. Morehead? This is Miss
Trimmerback from our office.

MISS TRIMMERBACK. How do you do?

MISS WATTS. She's a notary. We have some papers for Mrs.
Haines to sign.

MRS. MOREHEAD. Anything I can do?

MISS WATTS. The children will be with you? (*Mrs. Morehead
nods.*) Any incidental bills, Mrs. Morehead, send to the office. But
you understand, bills arriving after the divorce will be assumed by
Mrs. Haines under the terms of the settlement.

MRS. MOREHEAD. Mrs. Haines will be with you in a minute.
Please don't bother her with unnecessary details. She's—she's
pressed for time. (*Exits* R.)

MISS TRIMMERBACK. Gee, don't you feel sorry for Mrs.
Haines?

MISS WATTS. (*Bitterly.*) I don't feel sorry for any woman who
thinks the world owes her breakfast in bed.

MISS TRIMMERBACK. You don't like her.

MISS WATTS. Oh, she never interfered at the office.

MISS TRIMMERBACK. Maybe that's why he's been a success.

MISS WATTS. He'd have gotten further without her. Everything
big that came up, he was too cautious, because of her and the kids.
(*Opens brief-case, takes out papers and pen, arranges papers, for
signing, on table.*) Well, thank heavens it's almost over. He and I
can go back to work. (*Sits.*)

MISS TRIMMERBACK. What about Allen?

MISS WATTS. (*Guardedly.*) What about her?

MISS TRIMMERBACK. Is he going to marry her?

MISS WATTS. I don't butt into his private affairs. Oh, I hold no brief for Allen. But I must say knowing *her* gave him a new interest in his work. Before her, he was certainly going stale. That had me worried.

MISS TRIMMERBACK. (*Sinking on sofa.*) Well, she's lucky, I'll say.

MISS WATTS. Oh?

MISS TRIMMERBACK. I wish I could get a man to foot my bills. I'm sick and tired cooking my own breakfast, sloshing through the rain at 8 A. M., working like a dog. For what? Independence? A lot of independence you have on a woman's wages. I'd chuck it like that for a decent, or an indecent, home.

MISS WATTS. I'm sure you would.

MISS TRIMMERBACK. Wouldn't you?

MISS WATTS. I have a home.

MISS TRIMMERBACK. You mean Plattsburg, where you were born?

MISS WATTS. The office. That's my home.

MISS TRIMMERBACK. Some home! I see. The office-wife?

MISS WATTS. (*Defiantly.*) He could get along better without Mrs. Haines or Allen than he could without me.

MISS TRIMMERBACK. Oh, you're very efficient, dear. But what makes you think you're indispensable?

MISS WATTS. I relieve him of a thousand foolish details. I remind him of things he forgets, including, very often these days, his good opinion of himself. I never cry and I don't nag. I guess I *am* the office-wife. And a lot better off than Mrs. Haines. He'll never divorce me!

MISS TRIMMERBACK. (*Astonished.*) Why, you're in love with him! (*Both rise, face each other angrily.*)

MISS WATTS. What if I am? I'd rather work for him than marry the kind of a dumb cluck I could get— (*Almost tearful.*) just because he's a man— (*Enter Mary, L.*)

MARY. Yes, Miss Watts.

MISS WATTS. (*Collecting herself quickly.*) Here are the inventories of the furniture, Mrs. Haines. I had the golf cups, the books, etchings, and the ash stands sent to Mr. Haines' club. (*Pauses.*) Mr. Haines asked if he could also have the portrait of the two children.

MARY. (*Looking at blank space over mantel.*) Oh, but—

50

MISS WATTS. He said it wouldn't matter, if you really didn't care for him to have it.

MARY. It's in storage.

MISS WATTS. (*Laying paper on table.*) This will get it out. Sign there. The cook's letter of reference. Sign here. (*Mary sits, signs.*) The insurance papers. You sign here. (*Miss Trimmerback signs each paper after Mary.*) The transfer papers on the car. What do you want done with it?

MARY. Well, I—

MISS WATTS. I'll find a garage. Sign here. What do you want done if someone meets your price on this apartment?

MARY. Well, I thought—

MISS WATTS. This gives us power of attorney until you get back. Sign here.

MARY. But—I—

MISS WATTS. Oh, it's quite in order, Mrs. Haines. Now, Mr. Haines took the liberty of drawing you a new will. (*Places blue, legal-looking document before Mary.*)

MARY. (*Indignantly.*) But—really—

MISS WATTS. If anything were to happen to you in Reno, half your property would revert to him. A detail your lawyers overlooked. Mr. Haines drew up a codicil cutting himself out—

MARY. But I don't understand legal language, Miss Watts. I—I must have my lawyer—

MISS WATTS. As you please. (*Stiffly.*) Mr. Haines suggested this for *your* sake, not his. I'm sure you realize he has nothing but your interests at heart. (*A pause.*) Sign here. (*Mary signs, Miss Watts signs.*) We need three witnesses. (*Enter Jane, R., with box of flowers.*) Your maid will do.

MARY. Jane, please witness this. It's my will.

JANE. (*In tears.*) Oh, Mrs. Haines! (*Signs.*)

MISS WATTS. (*Gathering all the papers.*) You can always make changes, in the event of your remarriage. (*Mary rises.*) And don't hesitate to let me know at the office if there is anything I can ever do for you.

MARY. (*Coldly.*) There will be nothing, Miss Watts.

MISS WATTS. (*Cheerfully.*) Oh, there are always tag ends to a divorce, Mrs. Haines. And you know how Mr. Haines hates to be bothered with inconsequential details. Good day, Mrs. Haines, and pleasant journey to you! (*Exit Miss Watts, R., followed by Miss Trimmerback.*)

JANE. (*Sniveling as she places box on table.*) Mr. Haines said I was to give you these to wear on the train. (*Exits abruptly. Mary slowly opens box, takes out corsage of orchids and card. Reads aloud: "What can I say? Stephen." Then throws them violently in the corner. Enter Mrs. Morehead, little Mary, dressed for street.*)

MRS. MOREHEAD. All set, dear?

MARY. (*Grimly.*) All set— Mary, Mother wants to talk to you before she goes away.

MRS. MOREHEAD. Brother and I will wait for you downstairs. (*Exits Mrs. Morehead.*)

MARY. Mary, sit down, dear. (*Little Mary skips to sofa, sits down. A pause. Mary discovers it's going to be even more painful and difficult then she imagined.*) Mary—

LITTLE MARY. Yes, Mother?

MARY. Mary—

LITTLE MARY. (*Perplexed by Mary's tone, which she feels bodes no good to her.*) Have I done something wrong, Mother?

MARY. Oh, no, darling, no. (*She sits beside little Mary, and takes her hands.*) Mary, you know Daddy's been gone for some time.

LITTLE MARY. (*Sadly.*) A whole month.

MARY. Shall I tell you why?

LITTLE. MARY. (*Eagerly.*) Why?

MARY. (*Plunging in.*) You know, darling, when a man and woman fall in love what they do, don't you?

LITTLE MARY. They kiss a lot—

MARY. They get married—

LITTLE MARY. Oh, yes. And then they have those children.

MARY. Well, sometimes married people don't stay in love.

LITTLE MARY. What, Mother?

MARY. The husband and the wife—fall out of love.

LITTLE MARY. Why do they do that?

MARY. Well, they do, that's all. And when they do, they get unmarried. You see?

LITTLE. MARY. No.

MARY. Well, they do. They—they get what is called a divorce.

LITTLE MARY. (*Very matter of fact.*) Oh, do they?

MARY. You don't know what a divorce is, but—

LITTLE MARY. Yes, I do. I go to the movies, don't I? And lots of my friends have mummies and daddies who are divorced.

MARY. *(Relieved, kisses her.)* You know I love you very much, don't you, Mary?

LITTLE MARY. *(A pause.)* Of course, Mother.

MARY. Your father and I are going to get a divorce. That's why I'm going away. That's why — Oh, darling, I can't explain to you quite. But I promise you, when you are older you will understand. And You'll forgive me. You really will! Look at me, baby, please!

LITTLE MARY. *(Her lips begin to tremble.)* I'm looking at you, Mother — Doesn't Daddy love you any more?

MARY. No, he doesn't.

LITTLE MARY. Don't you love him?

MARY. I — I — no, Mary.

LITTLE MARY. Oh, Mother, why?

MARY. I — I don't know — But it isn't either Daddy's or Mother's fault.

LITTLE MARY. But, Mother, when you love somebody I thought you loved them until the day you die!

MARY. With children, yes. But grown-ups are different. They can fall out of love.

LITTLE MARY. I won't fall out of love with you and Daddy when I grow up. Will you fall out of love with me?

MARY. Oh, no, darling, that's different, too.

LITTLE MARY. *(Miserable.)* I don't see *how.*

MARY. You'll have to take my word for it, baby it is. This divorce has nothing to do with our love for you.

LITTLE MARY. But if you and Daddy —

MARY. *(Rising and drawing little Mary up to her.)* Darling, I'll explain it better to you in the taxi. We'll go alone in the taxi, shall we?

LITTLE MARY. But, Mother, if you and Daddy are getting a divorce, which one won't I see again? Daddy or you?

MARY. You and Brother will live with me. That's what happens when — when people get divorced. Children must go with their mothers. But you'll see Daddy — sometimes. Now, darling, come along.

LITTLE MARY. Please, Mother, wait for me downstairs.

MARY. Why?

LITTLE MARY. I have to go to the bathroom.

MARY. Then hurry along, dear— (*Sees orchids on floor, and as she moves to door, stoops, picks them up, goes out. Little Mary stands looking after her, stricken. Suddenly she goes to back of chair, hugs it, as if for comfort. Then she begins to cry and beat back of chair with her fists.*)

LITTLE MARY. Oh, please, please, Mother dear— Oh! Daddy, Daddy darling! Oh, why don't you do something—*do something*—Mother dear!

CURTAIN

ACT II

SCENE 1

A month later.
A room in a lying-in hospital. L., *a door to corridor.* R.,
a window banked to sill with expensive flowers. C., *a*
hospital bed, in which Edith, propped up in a sea of lace
pillows, lies with a small bundle at her breast. A white-
uniformed nurse sits by window. The droop of her shoul-
ders is eloquent: Edith is a trying patient. As curtain
rises, Edith reaches across bundle to bedside table for a
cigarette. She can't make it.

EDITH. (*Whining.*) Nurse!
NURSE. (*Rising wearily.*) Yes, Mrs. Potter.
EDITH. Throw me a cigarette.
NURSE. Can't you wait, at least until you're through nursing?
EDITH. How many children have you nursed? I've nursed four.
(*Nurse lights her cigarette, Edith shifts bundle slightly.*) Ouch!
Damn it! It's got jaws like a dinosaur. (*Enter Peggy with box of*
flowers.)
PEGGY. Hello, Edith.
EDITH. (*In a faint voice.*) Hello, Peggy.
PEGGY. (*Putting flowers on bed.*) Here—
EDITH. How thoughtful! Nurse, will you ask this damn hospital
if they're equipped with a decent vase? (*Nurse takes box, opens*
flowers and arranges them, with others, in window.)
PEGGY. (*Leans over baby.*) Oh, let me see. Oh, Edith, isn't he di-
vine!
EDITH. I hate that milky smell
PEGGY. (*Alarmed.*) What's that on his nose?
EDITH. What nose? Oh, that's an ash. (*Blows away ash. Hands*
Peggy a letter from bedside table.)
PEGGY. It's from Mary?
EDITH. (*Nodding.*) All about how healthy Reno is. Not a word
about how she feels. I thought she cared more about Stephen than

that. She sends her love to you and John. (*Peggy reads. The wail of a new-born is heard outside.*) Nurse, close that door. (*Nurse closes door.*) I can't tell you what that new-born yodel does to my nerves. (*To Peggy.*) What're you so down in the mouth about? I feel as badly about it as you do, but it was the thing Mary wanted to do, or she wouldn't have done it. Judging by that, she's reconciled to the whole idea.

PEGGY. She's just being brave!

EDITH. Brave? Why should she bother to be brave with her friends? Here, Nurse, he's through. (*Nurse takes bundle from her.*) I told Phelps to be sure to tell Stephen that Mary's perfectly happy. It will cheer Stephen up. He's been going around like a whipped dog.

PEGGY. Oh, Edith, please let me hold him! (*Nurse gives Peggy the baby.*)

NURSE. (*Smiling.*) Careful of his back, Mrs. Day.

PEGGY. (*Goes to window, hugging bundle.*) Oh, I like the feeling so!

EDITH. You wouldn't like it so much if you'd just had it. (*Whimpering.*) I had a terrible time, didn't I, Nurse?

NURSE. Oh, no, Mrs. Potter. You had a very easy time. (*She is suddenly angry.*) Why, women like you don't know what a terrible time is. Try bearing a baby and scrubbing floors. Try having one in a cold filthy kitchen, without ether, without a change of linen, without decent food, without a cent to bring it up—and try getting up the next day with your insides falling out, to cook your husband's—! (*Controls herself.*) No, Mrs. Potter, you didn't have a terrible time at all.—I'll take the baby, please. (*Sees reluctant expression on Peggy's face.*) I hope some day you'll have one of your own, Mrs. Day. (*Nurse exits with baby. Peggy breaks into tears.*)

EDITH. Well, for God's sake, Peggy, that old battle-axe didn't hurt my feelings a bit! They're all the same. If you don't get peritonitis or have quintuplets, they think you've had a picnic— (*Peggy sits beside bed, crying.*) What's the matter?

PEGGY. Oh, Edith—John and I are getting a divorce!

EDITH. (*Patting her hand.*) Well, darling, that's what I heard.

PEGGY. (*Surprised.*) But—but we didn't decide to until last night.

EDITH. (*Cheerfully.*) Oh, darling, everybody could see it was in the cards. Money, I suppose?

PEGGY. (*Nodding.*) Oh, dear! I wish Mary were here—

EDITH. Well, she'll be there. (*Laughs.*) Oh, forgive me, dear. I do feel sorry for you. But it is funny.

PEGGY. What's funny?

EDITH. It's gonna be quite a gathering of the clan. (*Sitting up in bed, full of energy to break the news.*) Howard Fowler's bounced Sylvia out right on her ear! He's threatened to divorce her right here in New York if she doesn't go to Reno. And name her young customer's man—

PEGGY. But—Howard's always known—

EDITH. Certainly. Howard hired him, so he'd have plenty of time for his own affairs. Howard's got some girl he wants to marry. But nobody, not even Winchell, knows who she is! Howard's a coony cuss. (*Laughing.*) I do think it's screaming. When you remember how Sylvia always thought she was putting something over on us girls! (*She laughs so hard, she gives herself a stitch. She falls back among her pillows, limp and martyred.*)

PEGGY. (*Bitterly.*) Life's awfully unattractive, isn't it?

EDITH. (*Yawning.*) Oh, I wouldn't complain if that damned stork would take the Indian sign off me.

CURTAIN

ACT II

Scene 2

A few weeks later. Mary's living room in a Reno hotel. In rear wall, a bay window showing a view of Reno's squat roof-tops and distant Nevada ranges. L., doors to kitchenette, bedroom. R., a door to corridor. A plush armchair, a sofa. In corner, Mary's half-packed trunks and bags. It is all very drab and ugly. As curtain rises, Lucy, a slatternly middle-aged, busky woman in a house-dress, is packing clothes that are strewn on armchair and table. She is singing in a nasal falsetto.

LUCY.

Down on ole Smokey, all covered with snow,

I lost my true lov-ver, from courtin' too slow.
Courtin' is pul-leasure, partin' is grief,
Anna false-hearted lov-ver is worse thanna thief—

(*Peggy enters, R. She wears a polo-coat and a wool tam. She is on the verge of tears.*)

PEGGY. Lucy, where's Mrs. Haines?

LUCY. Down waiting for the mail. You'll miss her a lot when she goes tomorrow? (*Peggy nods, sinks, dejected, on sofa.*) Mrs. Haines is about the nicest ever came here.

PEGGY. I hate Reno.

LUCY. You didn't come for fun. (*Goes on with her packing and singing.*)

The grave'll de-cay you, an' change you tuh dust,
Ain't one boy outta twenty, a poor gal kin trust—

PEGGY. You've seen lots of divorcees, haven't you, Lucy?

LUCY. Been cookin' for 'em for ten years.

PEGGY. You feel sorry for us?

LUCY. Well, ma'am, I don't. You feel plenty sorry enough for yourselves. (*Kindly.*) Lord, you ain't got much else to do.

PEGGY. (*Resentfully.*) You've never been married, Lucy.

LUCY. (*Indignant.*) I've had three—

PEGGY. Husbands?

LUCY. Kids!

PEGGY. Oh, then you're probably very happy—

LUCY. Lord, ma'am, I stopped thinking about being happy years ago.

PEGGY. You don't think about being happy?

LUCY. Ain't had the time. With the kids and all. And the old man such a demon when he's drinking— Them big, strong, red-headed men. They're fierce.

PEGGY. Oh, Lucy, he beats you? How terrible!

LUCY. Ain't it? When you think what a lot of women in this hotel need a beating worse than me.

PEGGY. But you live in Reno. You could get a divorce overnight.

LUCY. Lord, a woman can't get herself worked up to a thing like that overnight. I had a mind to do it once. I had the money, too. But I had to call it off.

PEGGY. Why?

LUCY. I found out I was in a family way. (*A rap on door.*)

PEGGY. (*Going to her.*) Lucy, tell Mrs. Haines I must talk to her

—alone—before supper— (*Enter Countess de Lage,* L. *She wears a gaudily checked riding habit, carries an enormous new sombrero and a jug of corn liquor.*)

COUNTESS. Ah, Peggy, how are you, dear child?

PEGGY. All right, Countess de Lage.

COUNTESS. I've been galloping madly over the desert all day. Lucy, here's a wee juggie. We must celebrate Mrs. Haines' divorce.

PEGGY. Oh, Countess de Lage, I don't think a divorce is anything to celebrate.

COUNTESS. Wait till you've lost as many husbands as I have, Peggy. (*Wistfully.*) Married, divorced, married, divorced! But where Love leads I always follow. So here I am, in Reno.

PEGGY. Oh, I wish I were anywhere else on earth.

COUNTESS. My dear, you've got the Reno jumpy-wumpies. Did you go to the doctor? What did he say?

PEGGY. He said it was—the altitude.

COUNTESS. Well, la, la, you'll get used to that. My third husband, Gustav, was a ski instructor. If one lives in Switzerland, Peggy, one has simply got to accept the Alps. As I used to say to myself, Flora, there those damn Alps are, and there's very little even you can do about it.

PEGGY. Yes, Countess de Lage. (*Exits, hurriedly,* L.)

COUNTESS. Oh, I wish she hadn't brought up the Alps, Lucy. It always reminds me of that nasty moment I had the day Gustav made me climb to the top of one of them. (*Sits in armchair.*) Lucy, pull off my boots. (*Lucy kneels, tugs at her boots.*) Anyhow, there we were. And suddenly it struck me that Gustav had pushed me. (*Tragically.*) I slid halfway down the mountain before I realized that Gustav didn't love me any more. (*Gaily.*) But Love takes care of its own, Lucy. I slid right into the arms of my fourth husband, the Count.

LUCY. (*Rises, with boots.*) Ain't that the one you're divorcing now?

COUNTESS. But of course, Lucy. (*Plaintively.*) What could I do when I found out he was putting arsenic in my Bromo Seltzer? Ah! L'amour! L'amour! Lucy, were you ever in love?

LUCY. Yes, ma'am.

COUNTESS. Tell me about it, Lucy.

LUCY. Well, ma'am, ain't much to tell. I was kinda enjoyin' the courtin' time. It was as purty a sight as you ever saw, to see him come lopin' across them hills. The sky so big and blue and that hair of his blazing like the be-jesuss in the sun. Then we'd sit on my back fence and spark. But, ma'am, you know how them big, strong, red-headed men are. They just got to get to the point. So we got married, ma'am. And natcherly, I ain't had no chanct to think about love since—

COUNTESS. (*She has not been listening.*) The trouble with me, Lucy, is I've been marrying too many foreigners. I think I'll go back to marrying Americans. (*Enter Miriam, R. without a mudmask. She is a breezy, flashy red-head, about 28, wearing a theatrical pair of lounging pajamas.*)

MIRIAM. Hya, Lucy?

LUCY. 'Evening, Mrs. Aarons. (*Exits R.*)

MIRIAM. Hya, Countess, how's rhythm on the range? (*Sees jug on table, pours Countess and herself drinks.*)

COUNTESS. Gallop, gallop, gallop, madly over the sagebrush! But now, Miriam, I'm having an emotional relapse. In two weeks I'll be free, free as a bird from that little French bastard. But whither, oh, whither shall I fly?

MIRIAM. To the arms of that comboy up at the dude ranch?

COUNTESS. (*Modestly.*) Miriam Aarons!

MIRIAM. Why, he's nuts for you, Countess. He likes you better than his horse, and it's such a damn big horse.

COUNTESS. (*Rises, and pads in her stocking-feet to sofa.*) Well, Buck Winston is nice. So young. So strong. Have you noticed the play of his muscles? (*Reclining.*) Musical. Musical.

MIRIAM. He could crack a cocoanut with those knees. If he could get them together. Say, Countess, that guy hasn't been arousing your honorable intentions in you, has he?

COUNTESS. Yes, Miriam, but I'm different from the rest of you. I've always put my faith in love. Still, I've had three divorces. Dare I risk a fourth?

MIRIAM. What are you risking, Countess, or maybe I shouldn't ask?

COUNTESS. I mean, Miriam, I could never make a success of Buck Winston at Newport.

MIRIAM. Even Mrs. Astor would have to admit Buck's handsome. If I had your dough, I'd take him to Hollywood first, then Newport.

COUNTESS. Hollywood? Why *not*? I might turn him into a picture star. After all, my second husband was a gondolier, and a month after I married him, a Duchess eloped with him. Ah! L'amour! (*Enter Sylvia*, R., *wearing smart dinner dress. Her trip to Reno has embittered but not subdued her.*)

MIRIAM. Hya, Sylvia? Going to a ball?

SYLVIA. (*Pours drink.*) Doing the town with a boy friend.

MIRIAM. Where'd you pick him up?

SYLVIA. The Silver State Bar. I'm not going to sit around moping, like Mary.

COUNTESS. Poor Mary. If her husband gave her the flimsiest excuse, she'd take him back.

SYLVIA. She has no pride. I'd roast in hell before I'd take Howard Fowler back. Kicking me out like that! After all I sacrificed!

MIRIAM. Such as what?

SYLVIA. I gave him my *youth!*

COUNTESS. (*Dreamily.*) Hélas, what else can a woman do with her youth but give it to a man?

MIRIAM. Hélas, she can't preserve it in alcohol.

COUNTESS. (*Practical.*) But, Sylvia, how could your husband kick you out, if you were a femme fidèle?

SYLVIA. Of course, I was a faithful wife. (*Miriam snorts.*) What are you laughing at?

MIRIAM. Two kinds of women, Sylvia, owls and ostriches. (*Raises her glass.*) To the feathered sisterhood! To the girls who get paid and paid. (*Parenthetically.*) And you got paid *plenty!*

SYLVIA. You bet I got plenty! The skunk! And I'd have got plenty more, if only I could have pinned something on him.

MIRIAM. Didn't you try?

SYLVIA. Certainly not. To put it mildly, Howard has been impotent for years!

COUNTESS. I never got a sou from any of my husbands except my first husband, Mr. Straus. He said the most touching thing in his will. I remember every word of it. "To my beloved wife, Flora, I leave all my estate in trust to be administered by executors, because she is an A No. 1 *schlemiel.*" (*Touched anew.*) Wasn't that sweet? (*Enter Mary*, R. *She is subdued. She is carrying some letters.*)

MIRIAM. Hya, queen?

MARY. Fine.

MIRIAM. Ya lie.

61

COUNTESS. Mary, I'm starved. (*Lucy enters,* L., *takes Mary's hat.*)

MARY. Supper's nearly ready. As my last official act in Reno, I cooked the whole thing with my hands, didn't I, Lucy?

LUCY. All but the steak and tomatoes and dessert, Mrs. Haines. (*Exits,* L.)

MARY. (*Gives letter to Sylvia, glancing, as she does so, at inscription.*) For you, Sylvia. From Edith?

SYLVIA. You couldn't miss that infantile scrawl. (*Pointedly.*) *You* didn't hear from anyone?

MARY. No.

SYLVIA. Well, darling, Stephen's hardly worth a broken heart.

MARY. The less you have to say about me and Stephen the better I like it!

SYLVIA. I'm only trying to cheer you up. That's more than you do for me.

MARY. I'm doing enough, just being pleasant to you.

SYLVIA. My, you have got the jitters, dear.

MIRIAM. Hey, Sylvia, we're all out here in the same boat. Mary's laid off you. Why don't you lay off her?

SYLVIA. Oh, I'm just trying to make her see life isn't over just because Stephen let her down. (*Opens her letter. A batch of press-clippings falls out. Countess picks them up, reads them idly, as Sylvia goes on with letter.*)

COUNTESS. You see, Miriam? What else is there for a woman but l'amour?

MIRIAM. There's a little corn whiskey left. (*She pours another drink.*)

COUNTESS. Cynic, you don't believe in Cupid.

MIRIAM. That double-crossing little squirt! Give me Donald Duck. (*To Mary.*) Have a drink? (*Mary shakes head.*) Listen, Babe, why not—relax? You'd feel better—

MARY. (*Laughing.*) Miriam, you're not very chatty about your own affairs.

COUNTESS. (*Suddenly engrossed by clippings from Sylvia's letter.*) Miriam, you sly puss, you never even breathed that you knew Sylvia's husband.

SYLVIA. (*Looking up from letter.*) What?

COUNTESS. (*Rises.*) Sylvia, listen to this from Winchell: "Miriam Vanities Aarons is being Renovated. Three guesses, Mrs. Fowler, for whose Ostermoor?" (*Sylvia snatches clippings from her.*)

MIRIAM. Why can't those lousy columnists leave a successful divorce alone?

COUNTESS. (*Reading another clipping.*) "Prominent stockbroker and ex-chorine to marry."

SYLVIA. (*To Miriam.*) Why, you dirty little hypocrite! (*During this, Peggy has entered and goes back of sofa. She listens but does not join group.*)

MARY. (*Going to her.*) Now, Sylvia—

SYLVIA. Did you know this?

MARY. No. But, Sylvia, why do you care? You don't love Howard—

SYLVIA. (*Brushing her aside.*) Love has nothing to do with it. She just wants Howard for his money!

MIRIAM. And what did you want him for? I made Howard pay for what he wants; you made him pay for what he doesn't want.

COUNTESS. Why Sylvia, I thought you said Howard was impotent? What a lovely surprise! Besides I'll stay bought. That's more than you did, Sylvia.

MIRIAM. If Howard's impotent, so is Ali Kahn.

SYLVIA. Why, you dirty little trollop!

MIRIAM. Don't start calling names, you Park Avenue push-over! (*Sylvia gives Miriam a terrific smack. In the twinkling of an eye, they are pulling hair. Mary seizes Sylvia's arm, Sylvia breaks loose. Countess tugs at Miriam's belt, as Lucy comes in, looks at fight with a rather professional eye, and exits for smelling-salts.*)

COUNTESS. Girls, girls, calmez-vous! (*Her interference enables Sylvia to slap Miriam unimpeded.*)

MIRIAM. (*Shoving the Countess on sofa.*) Out of the way, you fat old—! (*Sylvia grabs Miriam's hair.*) Ouch, let go! (*Sylvia is about to use her nails. Mary takes a hand.*)

MARY. I won't have this, you hear! (*Mary's interference allows Miriam to give Sylvia a terrific kick in the shins.*)

SYLVIA. (*Routed, in sobs.*) Ouch! You bitch, you! (*As she turns away, Miriam gives her another well-placed kick, which straightens Sylvia up.*)

MIRIAM. Take that! (*Sylvia, shrieking with rage and humiliation, grabs Miriam again, sinks her white teeth into Miriam's arm. At this mayhem, Mary seizes her, shakes her violently, pushes her sobbing into armchair.*)

MARY. (*To Miriam.*) That's enough.

MIRIAM. She's drawn blood!

MARY. There's iodine in the bathroom.

MIRIAM. Iodine? I need a rabies shot. (*Exits* R.)

SYLVIA. (*Blubbering, nursing her wounds.*) Oh, Mary, how could you let her do that to me!

MARY. (*Coldly.*) I'm terribly sorry, Sylvia.

SYLVIA. The humiliation! You're on her side. After all I've done for you!

MARY. What have you done for me?

SYLVIA. I warned *you!*

MARY. (*Bitterly.*) I'm not exactly grateful for that.

SYLVIA. (*Hysterical.*) Oh, aren't you? Listen to me, you ball of conceit. You're not the object of pity you suppose. Plenty of the girls are tickled to death you got what was coming to you. You deserved to lose Stephen, the stupid way you acted. But I always stood up for you, like a loyal friend. What thanks do I get? You knew about that woman, and you stood by gloating, while she—

MARY. Get out of here! (*Lucy enters from bedroom, with spirits of ammonia, as Sylvia gives way completely to hysteria, and, screaming with rage, picks up ash trays, glasses, and cigarette boxes, and hurls them violently against wall, while Lucy tries to get bottle under her nose.*)

SYLVIA. (*At top of her lungs.*) I hate you! I hate you! I hate everybody—

LUCY. (*Takes Sylvia firmly by shoulders, forces bottle under her nose.*) Listen, Mrs. Fowler! You got the hy-strikes! (*Rushes her gasping, sobbing, to door.*)

SYLVIA. You wait. Some day you'll need a woman friend. Then you'll think of me— (*Exit Lucy and Sylvia, struggling helplessly,* R.)

COUNTESS. (*Rising from sofa.*) Poor creatures. They've lost their equilibrium because they've lost their faith in love. (*Philosophically.*) L'amour. Remember the song Buck made up, just for me? (*Pours herself a drink, sings a cowboy song:*) "Oh, a man can ride a horse to the range above, But a woman's got to ride on the wings of love, Coma a ti-yi-yippi a yippi yi-yay." (*Throws jug over her shoulder, and exits* R., *still singing, as Miriam enters, the ravages of her fight repaired with a handkerchief.*)

MIRIAM. The coast clear?

PEGGY. Oh, that was the most disgusting thing I ever saw.

MIRIAM. Right, kid, we're a pair of alley cats—

MARY. You should not be here, Peggy, to see it at all. (*She picks up ash trays, etc.*)

MIRIAM. What the hell are you doing here?

MARY. John wanted to buy a car.

PEGGY. With my money! John couldn't afford a car.

MARY. But *you* could. What was his—is yours. What is yours—is your own. Very fair.

PEGGY. A woman's best protection is to keep a little money of her own.

MARY. A woman's best protection is—the right man. (*With gentle sarcasm.*) Obviously, John isn't the right man and Peggy will forget all about him in another month.

PEGGY. No, I won't. I can't. Because—because— (*Bursts into tears.*) Oh, Mary, I'm going to have a baby. Oh, Mary, what shall I do?

MARY. Peggy, what's his telephone number?

PEGGY. (*Quickly.*) Eldorado 5-2075. (*Miriam goes at once to phone. Gets operator, gives number.*) But oh, Mary, I can't tell him!

MIRIAM. Why? Isn't it his?

PEGGY. Oh, of course!

MIRIAM. And make it snappy, operator.

PEGGY. I always wanted it. But what can I do with it now?

MIRIAM. Land it with the Marines—

MARY. Peggy, you've shared your love with him. Your baby will share your blood, your eyes, your hair, your virtues—and your faults— But your little pin-money, that, of course, you could not share.

PEGGY. Oh, Mary, I know I'm wrong. But it's no use—you don't know the things he said to me. I have my pride.

MARY. (*Bitterly.*) Reno's full of women who all have their pride.

PEGGY. You think I'm like them.

MIRIAM. You've got the makings, dear.

MARY. Love has pride in nothing—but its own humility.

MIRIAM. (*At phone.*) Mr. Day, please. Reno calling—Mr. Day? My God, he must live by the phone. Just hold the— (*Peggy leaps to phone.*)

PEGGY. Hello, John. (*Clears her throat of a sob.*) No, I'm not sick. That is, I am sick! That is, I'm sick to my stomach. Oh, John! I'm going to have a baby— Oh, darling, are you?—Oh, darling, do you?—Oh, darling, so am I! So do I! 'Course, I forgive you.— Yes, precious. Yes, lamb. On the very next train! John? (*A kiss into phone. It is returned.*) Oh, Johnny, when I get back, things are going to be so different—! John, do you mind if I reverse the charges? (*Hangs up.*) I can't stay for supper. I've got to pack.

MARY. When you get back—don't see too much of your girl friends for a while.

PEGGY. Oh, I won't, Mary. It's all their fault we're here.

MARY. Not—entirely.

PEGGY. Good-bye! Oh, I'm so happy, I could cry. (*Exits R.*)

MIRIAM. Getting wise, aren't you?

MARY. Know all the answers.

MIRIAM. Then, why're you here?

MARY. I had plenty of advice, Miriam. (*Phone rings. Miriam goes to it.*)

MIRIAM. Hello. No, we completed that call, operator. (*Hangs up.*)

MARY. Cigarette?

MIRIAM. (*Suddenly.*) Listen.

MARY. There's nothing you can say I haven't heard.

MIRIAM. Sure? I come from a world where a woman's got to come out on top—or it's just too damned bad. Maybe I got a new slant.

MARY. (*Wearily.*) All right, Miriam. Talk to me about my— legal rights. Talk to me about security— What does it all come to? Compromise.

MIRIAM. What the hell? A woman's compromised the day she's born.

MARY. You can't compromise with utter defeat. He doesn't want me.

MIRIAM. How do you know?

MARY. How do I know—why else am I here?

MIRIAM. (*A pause. Then, mock-tragically.*) Because you've got no guts, Mary Haines. It happened to me—I lost my man, too.

MARY. (*Smiling.*) You?

MIRIAM. Oh, it only happened once. Got wise to myself after that. Look, how did I lose him? We didn't have enough dough to get married. I wouldn't sleep with him until we did. I had ideals—

66

God knows where I got 'em. I held out on him— (*Sighs.*) Can you beat it? I liked him a lot better than I've ever liked anybody since. What'd my Romeo do? Got himself another girl. I made a terrible stink. Why shouldn't I? I should. But what I ought not to have done was say—good-bye. I was like you.

MARY. I don't understand.

MIRIAM. Then get a load of this. I should of licked that girl where she licked me—in the hay.

MARY. Miriam!

MIRIAM. That's where you win the first round. And if I know men, that's still Custer's Last Stand. (*Mary walks away from her.*) Shocked you? You're too modest. You're ashamed. O. K., sister. But my idea of love is that love isn't ashamed of anything.

MARY. (*Turning to her.*) A good argument, Miriam. So modern. So simple. Sex the cause, sex the cure. It's too simple, Miriam. Your love battles are for—lovers—or professionals. (*Gently.*) Not for a man and woman who've been married twelve quiet years! Oh, I don't mean I wouldn't love Stephen's arms around me again. But I wouldn't recapture, if I could, our—young passion. That was the wonderful young thing we had. That was part of our youth, like the—babies. But not the thing that made him my husband, that made me his wife—Stephen *needed* me. He *needed* me for twelve years. Stephen doesn't need me any more.

MIRIAM. I get it. (*Phone rings.*) That's why I'm marrying this guy Fowler. He sure needs me. If I don't marry him he'll drink himself to death in a month, the poor dope.

MARY. (*At phone.*) Yes? No, operator, we completed— You say New York is calling Mrs. Haines? She'll take that call— (*To Miriam.*) Stephen!

MIRIAM. Listen, make him that speech you just made me!

MARY. (*Radiant.*) I knew he'd call. I knew when the last moment came, he'd realize he needed me.

MIRIAM. For God's sake, tell him that *you* need him!

MARY. Hello—hello? Stephen? Mary. Yes. I'm very cheerful. It's so good to hear your voice, Stephen. I— Why, yes, the final decree is granted tomorrow at 12—but, Stephen, I can— (*Frightened.*) But, Stephen! No—of course—I haven't seen the papers. How could I, out here? (*Long pause.*) Yes, I'd rather *you* told me. Of course I understand the position you're both in. No, I'm not bitter, not bitter at all— I—I hope you'll both be very happy. No,

67

I have no plans, no plans at all— Stephen, do you mind if I hang up? Good-bye, Stephen.—Good-bye—

MIRIAM. He's marrying her?

MARY. Tomorrow! Oh, God, why did I let this happen? We were married. We were one person. We had a good life. Oh, God, I've been a *fool!*

MIRIAM. Sure you have. Haven't we all, sister?

CURTAIN

ACT II

Scene 3

Early evening, two years later. Crystal's bathroom. L., a black marbleized tub with frilled shower-curtains. In a niche, back of tub, a gilded French phone. R., a satin-skirted dressing table, covered with glittering toilet bottles and cosmetic jars. Towel-racks piled with embroidered bath-towels. C., a door to Crystal's bedroom. As curtain rises, Crystal is lolling in the bath, reading a magazine, smoking, as Helene, a chic French maid enters.

HELENE. Madame has been soaking an hour.

CRYSTAL. *(Rudely.)* So what?

HELENE. But monsieur—

CRYSTAL. Monsieur is going out with me and my friends, whether he likes it or not. Has that kid gone home yet?

HELENE. Mademoiselle Mary has just finished the supper with her daddy. Madame, monsieur is so anxious that you say good night to her.

CRYSTAL. Listen, that kid doesn't want to bid me beddy-bye any more than I do. He's tried for two years to cram us down each other's throats. Let her go home to her mommer. *(Passes Helene a brush.)* Here—scrub— Some day I'm going to slap that kid down. She's too— *(As Helene scrubs too hard.)* Ow! You're taking my skin off— Oh, I'm so bored I could— *(Hurls the soap across the room.)* Helene, never marry a man who's deserted a "good woman." He's as cheerful as a man who's murdered his poor

68

old mother. (*Telephone rings.*) Get out! And, Helene, when Mrs. Fowler comes, keep her downstairs, if you have to sit on her. (*Exit Helene. Crystal picks up the telephone. Her voice melts.*) Hello, darling, I'm in the tub. I'm shrivelled to a peanut waiting for this call. No, I'm not afraid of a shock. You ought to know— Oh, Buck, I'm going to miss you like nobody's business. I can't tell you what it did to me, locking the door on our little apartment— I'll say we had fun! Coma ti-yi-yippy, what? Oh, no, say anything you like. This is the one place where I have some privacy. (*Crystal's back is to door. She does not hear a brief rap.*) Listen, baby, must you really go to the coast? Oh, the hell with Mr. Goldwyn. (*Enter little Mary. She stands hesitantly against the door.*) Listen, you don't have to tell me what you sacrificed to have a movie career. I've seen that cartoon you married. If Flora was ever a Countess, I'm the Duchess of Windsor. Well, Buck, maybe she's not such a half-wit, but— (*Sees little Mary.*) Oh—call me back in two minutes. I've had a small interruption. (*Hangs up.*) Who told you to come in here?

LITTLE MARY. (*Politely.*) Daddy. Good night. (*Turns to go.*)

CRYSTAL. (*Sweetly.*) Oh, don't go, darling. Hand me that brush.

LITTLE MARY. (*Gently.*) Please?

CRYSTAL. Please. (*Little Mary gives her brush.*)

LITTLE MARY. Good night. (*Goes to door.*)

CRYSTAL. My, you're in a hurry to tell Daddy about it.

LITTLE MARY. About what?

CRYSTAL. My talk on the telephone.

LITTLE MARY. I don't understand grown-ups on the telephone. They all sound silly. Good night.

CRYSTAL. Good night, who? (*A pause.*) You've been told to call me Aunty Crystal. (*A pause.*) Why don't you do it?

LITTLE MARY. (*Still edging to door.*) Yes.

CRYSTAL. Yes, what?

LITTLE MARY. (*Lamely.*) Yes, good night.

CRYSTAL. (*Angry.*) You sit down!

LITTLE MARY. Oh, it's awfully hot in here. I've got my coat on.

CRYSTAL. You heard me! (*Little Mary sits on stool before dressing table, squirms.*) We're going to have this out. I've done my damn—my level best to be friends with you, but you refuse to co-operate.

LITTLE MARY. What?

69

CRYSTAL. Co-operate.

LITTLE MARY. (*Nodding mechanically.*) Co-operate.

CRYSTAL. (*Exasperated.*) Answer my question. You don't like me. Why?

LITTLE MARY. (*Rising.*) Well, good night, Crystal—

CRYSTAL. I said, why?

LITTLE MARY. (*Very patiently.*) Listen, Crystal, my mother told me I wasn't to be rude to you.

CRYSTAL. For the last time, young lady, you give me one good reason why you don't like me.

LITTLE MARY. I never said I didn't like you, Crystal.

CRYSTAL. But you don't like me, do you?

LITTLE MARY. No, but I never *said* so. I've been very polite, Crystal, considering you're something awful!

CRYSTAL. Wait till your father hears this!

LITTLE MARY. (*Suddenly defiant.*) Listen— Daddy doesn't think you're so wonderful any more!

CRYSTAL. Did he tell you that?

LITTLE MARY. No. Daddy always pretends you're all right, but he's just ashamed to have Mother know what a mean, silly wife he's got. And I don't tell Mother what *we* think, because you've made her cry enough, Crystal. So I'm not going to co-operate *ever!*

CRYSTAL. Get out!

LITTLE MARY. (*Goes to door, then turns, rather superior.*) And *another* thing, I think this bathroom is perfectly ridiculous! Good night, Crystal! (*Exits. Phone rings. Crystal grabs it, irritable.*)

CRYSTAL. Yes, darling— That Haines brat. God, she gets under my skin!—No, she didn't hear anything. What good would it do her, anyhow? You're off in the morning, and Lord knows we've been discreet— What? You are? (*Giggling.*) Dining with the first Mrs. Haines?—Well, darling, lay off the gin. It makes you talk too much.—Well, just be careful, darling. (*Enter Sylvia, without knocking. She wears elaborate evening gown, and carries a cocktail. These two years have had no appreciable effect on Sylvia. She is her old Act 1 self again.*)

SYLVIA. Yoohoo! May I come in?

CRYSTAL. (*In phone.*) No, this is not the Aquarium. It's Grand Central Station. (*Hangs up.*)

SYLVIA. Who was that?

CRYSTAL. A wrong number.

SYLVIA. You were talking to a man.

CRYSTAL. Pass me that sponge.—Please.

SYLVIA. (*Waiting on Crystal.*) Oh, Crystal, you know you can trust me.

CRYSTAL. And that eye cup.

SYLVIA. There must be someone. After all, I've known Stephen for years. He's really not your type. I often wonder how you two got together. I was telling my psychoanalyst about it. You know, I've got to tell him everything.

CRYSTAL. That must be an awful effort.

SYLVIA. I don't mind discussing myself. But talking about my friends does make me feel disloyal. He says Stephen has a Guilt Complex.

CRYSTAL. What?

SYLVIA. (*Cheerfully.*) He says men of Stephen's generation were brought up to believe that infidelity is a sin. That's why he al lowed Mary to divorce him, and that's why he married you, Crys· tal. He had to marry you just to convince himself he was not a sexual monster.

CRYSTAL. Yes? Well, if Stephen is a sexual monster, psycho- analysis is through.

SYLVIA. And he says you've got a Cinderella Complex. He says most American women have. They're all brought up to believe that marriage to a rich man should be their aim in life. He says we neither please the men nor function as child-bearing animals—

CRYSTAL. (*Bored and angry.*) Will you function yourself into the bedroom?

SYLVIA. (*Hurt.*) I don't think that's the way to talk to me, after all I've done for you. When you married Stephen you didn't know a soul. It wasn't easy to put *you* over. Everybody was on Mary's side.

CRYSTAL. They still are. They never miss a chance to remind me what a noble, useful woman Mary has become since she left Stephen.

SYLVIA. (*Comforting.*) My dear, she's miserable! Why, she never sees a soul.

CRYSTAL. She's having a dinner party tonight.

SYLVIA. Edith told me. She's going. And Flora.

CRYSTAL. Flora?

SYLVIA. The Countess de Lage. Mrs. Buck Winston? My God, I

have to laugh when I think of Flora actually turning that cowboy into a movie star. Of course he's not my type, but he's positively the Chambermaid's Delight—

CRYSTAL. (*Fiercely.*) Will you shut up?

SYLVIA. But, Crystal—

CRYSTAL. I said shut up— (*Calling.*) Helene!

SYLVIA. Well, I think you're very ungrateful.

CRYSTAL. Well, take it up with your psychoanalyst. (*Helene enters.*) Helene, draw the curtains. I want to take a shower. (*Sylvia goes to door as Helene draws curtains.*) That's right, Sylvia—wait in the bedroom.

SYLVIA. (*Sees scales, decides to weigh herself.*) Oh, dear, I've lost another pound. I must remember to tell my analyst. You know, everything means something. (*Shower goes on. Helene exits. Sylvia gets off scales. During the following monologue, she goes to Crystal's dressing table, where she examines all the bottles and jars.*) But even my analyst says no woman should try to do as much as I do. He says I attach too much value to my feminine friendships. He says I have a Damon and Pythias Complex. I guess I have given too much of myself to other women. He says women are natural enemies— (*Picks up bottle.*) Why, Crystal, I thought you didn't touch up your hair— (*Sniffing perfume.*) My dear, I wouldn't use this. You smell it on every tart in New York. That reminds me— (*Going to shower-curtains.*) If you do have an affair, Crystal, for heaven's sake, be discreet. Remember what Howard did to me, the skunk. (*Peeking in.*) My, you're putting on weight. (*Going back to dressing table, she sits down, and begins to pry in all the drawers.*) But men are so mercenary. They think they own you body and soul, just because they pay the bills— I tried this cream. It brought out pimples— Of course, Crystal, if you were smart, you'd have a baby. It's the only real hold a woman has— (*Helene enters.*)

HELENE. Monsieur says will madame be long?

SYLVIA. Can't you see she's rushing?— (*Helene exits. Shower goes off.*) Men are so selfish! When you're only making yourself beautiful for them. (*Opens another drawer.*) I wish I could find a man who would understand my need for a companion— (*Finds a key, examines it.*) Why, Crystal, what are you doing with a key to the Gothic Apartments? (*Crystal's head pops from behind curtain.*)

CRYSTAL. What?—Oh— (*Nervously.*) Oh, that! (*Playing for time.*) Throw me a towel, Sylvia!
SYLVIA. (*Bringing her towel.*) That's where Howard had me followed. The doorman there is a professional blackmailer! (*Crystal has wrapped herself in a big towel, now steps from behind shower-curtain and sits on rim of tub to dry her legs.*) I asked my psycho-analyst about him, and he said blackmailers are really perverts who can't think of a good perversion. So they blackmail people instead.
CRYSTAL. (*Going to dressing table.*) Really? Well, he can't blackmail me now. (*As she passes Sylvia, she lightly snatches key from her.*) The Gothic Apartments are where Stephen and I had to go, before the divorce. I keep it for sentimental reasons. (*Smiling, she drops key back in drawer, locks it.*)
SYLVIA. Poor Stephen! My dear, I thought tonight how tired he looked, and old. Crystal, I've told you everything. Tell me: how long do you think you can be faithful to Stephen?
CRYSTAL. (*Making up her face.*) Well, life plays funny tricks. The urge might hit me tomorrow.
SYLVIA. I doubt it, pet. You're a typical blonde.
CRYSTAL. So what?
SYLVIA. (*Loftily.*) Most *blondes* are frigid.
CRYSTAL. Really? Well, maybe that's just a dirty piece of *brunette* propaganda!

CURTAIN

ACT II

Scene 4

11 o'clock the same night. Mary's bedroom. A charming, simple room. L., a door to dressing-room. R., a door to hall. As curtain rises, Jane is arranging a number of evening wraps on the bed. Miriam, Mary and Nancy are entering.

MIRIAM. Thanks, baby, a lot! I never was at a wetter dinner.
MARY. It was a success. I left Reno two years ago today. This was a memorial dinner for you old Renoites, and your new husbands.

MIRIAM. I get it. Listen, there's no soap eating out your heart, sister!

NANCY. Mary, if I had a heroine in one of my books who behaved the way you do, my two readers would never believe it. No one man is worth it.

MIRIAM. Say, the whole Racquet Club's not worth it— Speaking of my dear husband Howard—the skunk—can I have a whiskey and soda?

NANCY. Make it two. (*Jane exits* R.)

MIRIAM. I lay off when Howard's around. I'm weaning him from the bottle by easy stages. He's in the secondary stage now.

NANCY. What stage is that?

MIRIAM. He puts ice in.

MARY. How's matrimony, Miriam? Making a go of it?

MIRIAM. I'm doing a reconstruction job that makes Boulder Dam look like an egg-cup. (*Enter Peggy*, R.)

PEGGY. Oh, Mary, can't we get off to the party? I have to get home early. Little John always wakes up. Little John said the cutest thing the other day. (*A dramatic pause.*) He said da-da—!

NANCY. When does he enter Columbia? (*Enter Jane with tray and highballs.*)

MARY. Jane, tell Mrs. Winston the ladies are ready to go.

JANE. Mrs. Winston, ma'am, is drinking with the gentlemen.

MARY. Well, tell her to come up. (*Exit Jane.*)

MIRIAM. What's the hurry? Two more snootfuls, and Flora will float up on her own breath. (*Enter Edith*, R.)

EDITH. (*Petulantly.*) Mary, I wish you had an elevator in this house. It's so difficult to walk upstairs in my condition.

MARY. Edith, are you Catholic or just careless?

EDITH. Mary, isn't this your old furniture?

MARY. Yes.

EDITH. I think you should get rid of it. There's nothing that keeps a woman so in the dumps as sleeping in a bed with old associations. Mary, you're carrying this nunnery business too far. How do you expect to find anyone else, if you don't make an effort?

MARY. I don't want anyone, Edith. (*Mock cynical.*) I hate men! Men are awful—

EDITH. Oh, they're not all like Stephen, dear.

MARY. I saw plenty of men when I came back from Reno. They're

74

all alike. They never leave you at your own front door without a wrestling-match.

MIRIAM. It beats me how, in a taxi, the nicest guy turns into Harpo Marx.

EDITH. You know I asked Phelps about that once. I said, "Why does a man always act like a Don Juan in a taxi?" And he said it was a hang-over from their bachelor days when a man's sex life was conditioned by the click of the meter. Mary, want to hear something about Sylvia? (*Mary, Miriam, Nancy and Peggy: chorus, "No!"*) Well, Sylvia's going to a psychoanalyst. She says you destroyed all her faith in friendship.

MARY. As if any woman needed to go to a psychoanalyst to find out she can't trust women.

EDITH. Mary, you've grown awfully cynical.

MARY. Isn't "wise" the word? I'm beginning to understand women.

NANCY. Too bad! That's the beginning of woman's inhumanity to woman.

EDITH. (*Moving to door,* L.) Oh, they're going to talk philosophy, Peggy. Come on in here while I powder my nose.

PEGGY. Edith, did I tell you how little John said (*A breathless pause.*) da-da?

EDITH. Listen, I wouldn't care if *this* one was born reading Shakespeare! (*They exit, as enter Mrs. Morehead, in street clothes,* R.)

MRS. MOREHEAD. Oh, hello, girls! Hello, dear. Party over?

MARY. Enjoy the movies, Mother?

MRS. MOREHEAD. I wish I could make up my mind whether or not I like the Beatles. (*Enter Countess de Lage,* R. *She is a tangle of tulle and jewels. She has a slight "edge" on.*)

COUNTESS. Such a lovely dinner! It's so wonderful to see all our lives temporarily settled!

MARY. My mother, Mrs. Morehead, Mrs. Winston. Mrs. Buck Winston.

MRS. MOREHEAD. (*Trying to place the name.*) Buck Winston?

MARY. The movie star.

MRS. MOREHEAD. Ah, yes! (*Pleasantly.*) My granddaughter adores your son on the screen.

COUNTESS. (*Good-naturedly.*) I daresay the public does see Buck as just a boy. And it is a trifle absurd *me* being married to a

75

movie star. But, Mrs. Morehead, you wouldn't believe how many of my Newport friends who ridiculed Buck when I married him positively claw for invitations to Hollywood. Mais là, East is East and West is West, but I always say Le Cinema is the Great Leveller!

MRS. MOREHEAD. You don't say! (*Edges to hall door.*)

COUNTESS. Mrs. Morehead, do whip into something and come along with Mary to my party. The Casino Roof. Everyone's clamored to come. I have no idea who's going to be there.

MRS. MOREHEAD. Well, you're sure to know somebody. (*To Mary.*) Later, dear? (*Mary nods, Mrs. Morehead escapes, R.*)

COUNTESS. (*Gathering her wrap.*) Mary, you're not coming?

MARY. I'm very tired, Flora.

COUNTESS. Oh, you're cross because Buck's had a wee droppie.

MIRIAM. Don't be modest, Flora. Your groom is stinko.

COUNTESS. I do wish he wouldn't drink straight gin. You know, he's not allowed to. Mr. Zanuck put that in the new contract.

MIRIAM. Countess, you should have all your marriage contracts drawn up by Mr. Zanuck.

COUNTESS. Mary, do come. This is *really* our farewell party. I'm never coming back to New York.

MARY. What's wrong with New York, Flora?

COUNTESS. (*Whispering.*) Mary, can I trust you?

MARY. Of course, Flora!

COUNTESS. (*To others.*) You will keep this just between the four of us?

MIRIAM. Shoot, Flora, it's a nationwide hookup!

COUNTESS. (*Settling herself beside Mary on foot of bed.*) Well, you know how Buck was? (*Wistfully.*) So—so impassioné?

MIRIAM. That boy had something.

COUNTESS. (*Tartly.*) Well, he hasn't got it any more, Miriam! First, I thought it was just gin, interfering with his libido— (*Tearfully.*) But now I think Buck is deceiving me—

NANCY. How incredible!

COUNTESS. Well, I have no proof. Except he comes home every afternoon smelling of a strange perfume.

MARY. Where does he say he's been?

COUNTESS. Visiting his horse. But Trixie was shipped to Hollywood last week. You remember, I was photographed with her in the baggage-car? Now he says he's been going to the Grand Central Gymnasium. But I telephoned today. Some great oaf answered. I said: "Is Buck Winston there?" He said: "Who? No." So I said: "My dear good man, he comes every day." So he said: "My mistake, lady, he's inside now boxing with James Bond."

MARY. Poor Flora!

COUNTESS. (*Practical.*) That's why I think it's safer just to keep floating around.

MARY. I understand—l'amour.

COUNTESS. L'amour, yes, but jamais, (*She has her lucid moments.*) jamais *lopsided* amour!

MARY. (*Laughing.*) Lopsided amour is better than no amour at all. Flora, let him make a fool of you. Let him do anything he wants, as long as he stays. He's taking the trouble to deceive you. (*Half to herself.*) And if he took the trouble, he really must have cared—

NANCY. The Voice of Experience.

MIRIAM. (*To Countess.*) Come on, chin up.

NANCY. That's right. Both of them! (*Enter Peggy and Edith.*)

COUNTESS. (*Rising.*) Oh, cheries, you missed it! I was just saying—now you will keep this just among the six of us?—I suspect Buck of being unfaithful. Of course, it's my own fault. I should have had him watched. The way I did all the others. I wish I'd found out where he's had that apartment!

PEGGY. An apartment—?

COUNTESS. Where would you expect him to go? Central Park? Why, it's winter.

PEGGY. Oh, I've always heard people went to hotels.

COUNTESS. But, cherie, *Buck* couldn't go to a hotel. You know what would happen. At the most inopportune moment someone would say: "Mr. Winston, may I have your autograph?" It happened to us on our wedding night. I would have sent for the manager, but it was the manager asking for the autograph. (*Exits R.*)

EDITH. (*Getting her wrap.*) Darling, you really won't come to Flora's party?

MARY. No, Edith!

EDITH. Then I can tell you. Of course, I know how you feel about your Ex—and his New Deal—though I think you'd be glad he's so happy.

MARY. I am.

EDITH. Sylvia telephoned tonight. She and Crystal and Stephen are going on to the Roof with a theatre party. Well, darling, I don't feel much like going myself. I loathe this dress. My husband says I look as though I were going to sing Wagner in it. (*Exits* R.)

NANCY. Think I'll go, too, Mary! It's a good chance to study Park Avenue's flora and fauna. And I'm writing a new book. It's called "Gone with the Ice-man," or "Sex Has No Place in the Home." (*Exits with Peggy.*)

MIRIAM. (*To Mary.*) Listen, Queen, change your mind! Let's go on to the party!

MARY. No, Miriam.

MIRIAM. Well, I'm going. Wish you could see the cooing-fest Howard and I put on for Sylvia— Shall I spit in Crystal's eye for you? (*Mary shakes her head.*) You're passing up a swell chance, sister! Where I spit no grass grows ever! (*Exits. Jane enters, R. Mary begins to unfasten her dress, takes off her jewels, lays them on dresser.*)

MARY. Jane, turn down my bed.

JANE. Yes, ma'am. (*Mary goes into boudoir, L.*)

MARY. (*Off stage.*) Did Mary have a nice time with her father?

JANE. (*Turning down bed.*) Well, ma'am, you know how she is when she comes home.

MARY. (*Off stage.*) I'm afraid she's never going to get used to it.

JANE. She takes after you, ma'am, if you'll pardon me. Always brooding. Sometimes, ma'am, I think it would be better if she didn't see her father. Or maybe, ma'am—though it's none of my business—if you could find some nice man— (*Enter Mrs. Morehead, R., in wrapper and slippers.*)

MRS. MOREHEAD. Going to bed, darling?

MARY. (*Off stage.*) Yes, Mother.

MRS. MOREHEAD. Shall we chat for a moment? Jane, I'll have a cigarette.

JANE. (*Surprised.*) Mrs. Morehead!

MRS. MOREHEAD. Those dreadful women made me nervous. Why Mrs. Haines tolerates them even once a year is beyond me!

MARY. (*Entering, in a nightgown.*) An object lesson. Smoking, Mother?

MRS. MOREHEAD. Oh, you, too?

MARY. Me too?

MRS. MOREHEAD. I just felt your father give me a spooky pinch.

You'd think after ten years his ghost might have grown more tolerant.

JANE. Good night, ma'am. (*Switches off side-lights.*)

MARY and MRS. MOREHEAD. Good night, Jane. (*Exit Jane. Mary gets into bed, opens book, flips through it.*)

MRS. MOREHEAD. (*Sitting on bed.*) Good book?

MARY. Don't know. Nancy just gave it to me. It's about—love. Poetry. All about love. (*Reads.*) "When love beckons to you, follow him, though his ways are hard and steep. And when his wings enfold you, yield to him— Though his voice may shatter your dreams as the North Wind lays waste the garden."

MRS. MOREHEAD. Well, all I can say is, that's very tactless of Nancy. (*Suddenly.*) Oh, Mary, I wish you could find—

MARY. (*Slams book shut.*) Some nice man. We've been all over that before, Mother. I had the only one I ever wanted, I lost him—

MRS. MOREHEAD. It wasn't entirely your fault.

MARY. If I hadn't listened to everyone, everything but my own heart!

MRS. MOREHEAD. He loved her.

MARY. He still does. Though you know, Mother, I'm just beginning to doubt it.

MRS. MOREHEAD. Why?

MARY. Because so many people, like Edith, make a point of telling me how much he loves her. Oh, Mother, I'm terribly tired.

MRS. MOREHEAD. Well, do cheer up, darling. Living alone has its compensations. You can go where you please, wear what you please and eat what you please. I had to wait twenty years to order the kind of meal I liked! Your father called it bird-food— And, heaven knows, it's marvelous to be able to sprawl out in bed, like a swastika. Good night, darling.

MARY. Good night, Mother.

MRS. MOREHEAD. Don't read by that light. You'll hurt your eyes. (*Exits. Mary props herself against pillows, begins to read. Enter little Mary, in nightgown, barefooted, very sleepy.*)

LITTLE MARY. Mother?

MARY. Darling, what's the matter?

LITTLE MARY. (*Goes to bed.*) I had a bad dream!

MARY. Darling, what was it?

LITTLE MARY. I forget. Let me crawl in with you, Mother.

MARY. (*Helping her in.*) I'm so restless.

LITTLE MARY. I don't mind if you kick me. You know, that's the only good thing about divorce; you get to sleep with your mother. (*She kisses her. A pause.*) I taste lipstick.

MARY. I haven't washed yet. Good night, darling.

LITTLE MARY. You know, you're a very sympathetic mother.

MARY. Am I?

LITTLE MARY. Oh, yes. So would you just tickle my back?

MARY. All right. But go to sleep— (*A pause.*)

LITTLE MARY. She's so silly!

MARY. Who?

LITTLE MARY. Crystal.

MARY. Ssh—

LITTLE MARY. I told Daddy so tonight.

MARY. Oh, you mustn't hurt Daddy's feelings.

LITTLE MARY. Mother?

MARY. Sssh!

LITTLE MARY. I think Daddy doesn't love her as much as you any more.

MARY. What makes you think so, Mary?

LITTLE MARY. He told me so after I saw Crystal.

MARY. What?

LITTLE MARY. But he said I mustn't tell you because, naturally, why do you care how he feels. (*A pause.*) Oh, don't stop tickling, Mother. (*A pause.*) Mother?

MARY. Yes?

LITTLE MARY. What's anyone want with a telephone in the bathroom?

MARY. I don't know. Sssh!

LITTLE MARY. Crystal has one. She was awful mad when I walked in on her while she was talking.

MARY. Sleep, Mary!

LITTLE MARY. Mother, who's the Duchess of Windsor?

MARY. What a question!

LITTLE MARY. Well, Crystal said on the telephone if somebody else was a Countess, she was the Duchess of Windsor!

MARY. Really!

LITTLE MARY. Good night, Mother.

MARY. Good night, baby. (*A pause.*)

LITTLE MARY. I wonder if it was the same man you had for dinner.

MARY. Maybe, ssh!

LITTLE MARY. I thought so.

MARY. (*Curiously.*) If who was the same man?

LITTLE MARY. Crystal was talking to, so lovey-dovey.

MARY. (*Protestingly.*) Oh, Mary!

LITTLE MARY. Well, the front part was the same, Mother.

MARY. (*A pause.*) The front part of what?

LITTLE MARY. His name, Mother!

MARY. (*Taking her by shoulders.*) What are you talking about?

LITTLE MARY. That man Crystal was talking to in the bathtub.

MARY. (*Half shaking her.*) Mary, what do you mean?

LITTLE MARY. I mean his front name was Buck, Mother! (*Mary gets quickly out of bed, rings bell on table.*) Oh, Mother, what are you doing?

MARY. Go to sleep, darling. (*Begins to pull on her stockings.*)

LITTLE MARY. Grown-ups are so sudden. Are you dressing?

MARY. Yes, Mary.

LITTLE MARY. You forgot you were invited to a party?

MARY. Almost, Mary.

LITTLE MARY. What are you going to do when you get there, Mother?

MARY. I don't know yet. But I'm going to do something.

LITTLE MARY. Well, have a good time! (*Rolls over. Then suddenly sits up.*) Mother!

MARY. Yes?

LITTLE MARY. I remember now I had something to tell you!

MARY. (*Eagerly.*) Yes?

LITTLE MARY. (*Dolefully.*) I was awfully rude to Crystal.

MARY. I'll forgive you this time. (*Enter Jane.*)

JANE. You ring, ma'am?

MARY. Yes. My evening dress, Jane, and a taxi—and don't stand there gaping! Hurry! Hurry!

CURTAIN

ACT II

Scene 5

*Later, the same night. Powder Room at the Casino Roof.
The decoration is rich, tawdry and modernistic. R., a
swinging door from lobby. L., another to the washrooms.
The rest of the wall-space, L. and R., is taken up by
counter-like dressing tables and mirrors. Rear wall is a
great window overlooking the glitter of midnight Man-
hattan. An overstuffed sofa and an armchair upholstered
in modernistic fabric. Near the door, R., a screen hides
the coat-rack. By this, a chair for Sadie, a little old woman in a black maid's uniform and apron. As curtain rises,
Sadie is reading a tabloid, which she puts down when two
flashily dressed girls enter from lobby. They check their
wraps.*

1ST GIRL. It's jammed.

2ND GIRL. Oh, my boy-friend'll get a table. (*Enter two society
women. They move directly across stage to washroom.*)

1ST WOMAN. My dear, won't he let you?

2ND WOMAN. No, he won't.

1ST WOMAN. How incredibly foul!

2ND WOMAN. I'm heartbroken. But I have to be philosophical;
after all, missing one winter in Palm Beach really won't kill me.
(*Enter "Cigarettes," a pretty girl in white satin blouse and short
black skirt. Carries tray of cigarettes.*)

1ST GIRL. (*Moving L.*) Thought you and the boy friend had a
row?

2ND GIRL. We did.

1ST GIRL. What about?

2ND GIRL. His wife.

1ST GIRL. His wife? What right has she got to butt in?

2ND GIRL. He's got some cockeyed idea that after twenty years
he can't kick her out. (*They exit L.*)

CIGARETTES. Jeepers, why don't they get sick of this joint night
after night! Same music, same act, same faces.

SADIE. They like familiarity. It gives them confidence.

CIGARETTES. I'll say they like familiarity. Most of them shoving around that floor would be more comfortable with each other in bed.

SADIE. In bed? If they was to get that over, what would they use for conversation? (*Enter a Dowager and a Debutante,* R. *They move directly across stage.*)

DOWAGER. —dancing like that! What can those boys think of you?

DEBUTANTE. (*Wearily.*) Oh, Mother.

DOWAGER. Guzzling champagne like that! After all I spent on your education!

DEBUTANTE. Oh, Mother.

DOWAGER. It's one thing to come out. It's quite another to go under the table! (*They exit,* L.)

SADIE. —Getting married, dearie?

CIGARETTES. (*Sinking, very tired, on arm of a chair.*) As soon as Mike gets a job. It ain't fair! Why, we could get married and have a family on that coat— Sadie, wh'd'ya say if I was to tell you I'm a Commyanist?

SADIE. I'd say ya was bats. I was a Norman Thomas fan. Where'd it get me? (*Enter Countess, piloted by Nancy and Miriam. She is tight and tearful. Miriam and Nancy get her, with some difficulty, to the sofa.*)

COUNTESS. (*Tacking.*) How could Buck do such a thing to me! Oh, the Dr. Jekyll! The Mr. Hyde! Which was which?

MIRIAM. Pipe down or you'll put an awful dent in his career, Flora.

COUNTESS. What of my career? I've had five husbands. Buck's the first one who ever told me what he really thought of me—in public.

NANCY. It takes all kinds of husbands to round out a career like yours, Flora.

COUNTESS. He told me he'd been deceiving me for months. Right in the middle of "Smoke Gets in Your Eyes." (*Kicks off shoes.*) Oh, I feel so—superfluous!

MIRIAM. (*To Sadie.*) A bromo-seltzer.

COUNTESS. Bromo-seltzer? Qu'-est-que c'est que ca?

NANCY. It will settle your—superfluity. Flora, did he tell you the lady's name?

COUNTESS. (*Indignant.*) Unfortunately, Nancy, he's not that drunk.

MIRIAM. (*As Sadie exits,* R.) And another drink for Mr. Winston!

COUNTESS. No, Miriam. He wouldn't tell me her name, because she's a married woman. Buck is very proletarian. He just said *she* was a natural blonde.

NANCY. That ought to narrow down the field.

COUNTESS. He said she was pretty as a painted wagon.

MIRIAM. Oh, you're a pretty damned colorful Calliope yourself. Snap out of it, Flora. You know, you're going to forgive him.

COUNTESS. (*Firmly.*) I'd forgive unfaithfulness, but not base ingratitude. I rescued him from those prairies. I married him. What thanks do I get? (*Wailing.*) He says he'll be a cockeyed coyote if he'll herd an old beef like me back to the coast!

NANCY. Let this be your lesson. Don't let your next husband become financially independent of you.

COUNTESS. Now, don't lecture me, Nancy. Every time I marry I learn something. This has taught me once and for all—you can't expect *noblesse oblige* from a cowboy— (*Sitting up.*) Ohhh, my eyes! They're full of mascara.

NANCY. (*Helping her off couch. To Miriam.*) We've got to get her home. I'll get Buck and meet us in the lobby. We're headin' for the last round-up! (*Nancy exits* R.)

COUNTESS. No. There's a telephone in there. And I'm going to call up Mr. Zanuck.

MIRIAM. Now, Flora, what can he do?

COUNTESS. I just want to remind him he can't make a picture with Buck until I say so.

MIRIAM. Why not?

COUNTESS. I own Buck's horse! (*Miriam gives a cowboy yell, slaps Countess on back. They exit to Ladies' Room as Sadie, with a bromo-seltzer, enters* R., *followed by Cigarettes.*)

CIGARETTES. What's it all about?

SADIE. (*Picks up Countess' shoes, as she crosses* L.) One gets you ten—some man.

CIGARETTES. Bet he isn't worth it.

SADIE. You can always collect on that one. (*Exits* L., *as re-enter,* L., *Dowager and Debutante.*)

DOWAGER. —Laughing and joking with those boys like that!

DEBUTANTE. Yes, Mother.

DOWAGER. What can they think of you?

84

DEBUTANTE. Yes, Mother.

DOWAGER. And don't think I didn't overhear that Princeton boy call me an old drizzle-puss, either! (*Exits* R.)

SADIE. (*Enters,* L., *to Cigarettes.*) She wants gin in her bromo-seltzer. (*Enter Mary* R. *and Miriam* L.)

MIRIAM. (*Protesting.*) Crystal's not in there. I don't think she's in the joint.

MARY. She's coming. I know it.

MIRIAM. So what are you going to do when you find her? (*Sadie takes Mary's wrap.*)

MARY. I don't know. But I've got to find her tonight. Buck's going to Hollywood in the morning.

MIRIAM. Say, why don't you settle this matter with Stephen?

MARY. I have no proof, I tell you! But if Buck is as drunk as you say, he'll give away something.

MIRIAM. Listen, he's been trying all night to give Flora away to the doorman. Got a twenty-dollar bill?

MARY. Yes.

MIRIAM. That'll get Buck locked in the men's room till we need him. (*Exits,* R., *with Mary, as enter,* L., *the two society women. They cross the stage.*)

1ST WOMAN. Not three pounds?

2ND WOMAN. Three pounds!

1ST WOMAN. How divine! Aren't you ecstatic?

2ND WOMAN. Yes, but it's the moral satisfaction. Just bananas and milk for one whole week! That called for enormous character! (*They exit,* R.)

CIGARETTES. (*To Sadie.*) Comes the Revolution, she'll diet plenty. (*Enter Peggy and Edith,* R. *They powder, at mirror,* R.)

PEGGY. I wish I hadn't come.

EDITH. Well, your husband didn't want you to.

PEGGY. (*Goes for her wrap.*) Flora was disgusting!

EDITH. But it was funny. Even the kettle drummer was laughing. (*Sadie gives Edith and Peggy their wraps.*)

EDITH. My dear, who could stand the life we lead without a sense of humor? But Flora is a fool. Always remember, Peggy, it's matrimonial suicide to be jealous when you have a really good reason.

PEGGY. Edith, don't you ever get tired of giving advice?

EDITH. Listen, Peggy, I'm the only happy woman you know. Why? I don't ask Phelps or any man to understand me. How could he? I'm a woman. (*Pulls down her corset.*) And I don't try to understand them. They're just animals. Who am I to quarrel with the way God made them? I've got security. And I say: "What the hell?" And let nature take its course—it's going to, anyway. (*They exit, R., as enter the 2 girls, L.*)

2ND GIRL. (*Powdering at mirror, L.*) —So there we were on Sattiday night and it's Atlantic City. And he says: "I gotta go home tomorrow, baby!" And I says: (*Pulls up her stockings.*) "Why dja got to?" And he says: "My wife always expects me home on Easter Sunday." So I says: "What's she expect ya to do? Lay an egg?"

1ST GIRL. They got no sentiment. (*Enter, R., a girl, in distress. The shoulder strap of her very low décolletage has broken.*)

GIRL IN DISTRESS. (*To Sadie.*) Have you got a safety pin? I was never so embarrassed! (*Sadie gets pin.*)

2ND GIRL. (*Crossing, R.*) So I told him, "I had a great career until you made me give up the stage, you lunkhead. For what? A couple of cheesy diamond bracelets? A lousy car, which every time it breaks down you got to have the parts shipped over from Italy." (*Girls exit.*)

GIRL IN DISTRESS. (*Clutching right breast.*) It practically popped out into the soup. So my escort says, "Don't look now, you've just dropped something!" If only it had been the left one. It's so much better. (*Enter Crystal and Sylvia, R. They move to check their wraps with Sadie.*)

SADIE. Just a minute, please. (*They go to mirror, L.*)

SYLVIA. Stephen is in a mood.

CRYSTAL. He can take it and like it.

GIRL IN DISTRESS. (*To Sadie.*) Does it show now?

SADIE. Not what it did before, miss.

GIRL IN DISTRESS. Thank you. (*She exits, R. Sadie takes Crystal's and Sylvia's wraps.*)

CRYSTAL. Is my mouth on straight?

SYLVIA. Crystal, you didn't come here to see somebody, did you?

CRYSTAL. Oh, Sylvia, can't you lay off that for a minute? (*Enter Mary and Miriam, L.*)

MARY. (*Moving forward resolutely.*) Mrs. Haines, this is a great pleasure!

CRYSTAL. (*Turning.*) I beg your pardon?

MARY. Such a lovely party! I was afraid you weren't coming.

86

(*Introducing Crystal and Miriam and Sylvia.*) Mrs. Fowler, Mrs. Haines, Mrs. Fowler, Mrs. Fowler.

MIRIAM. (*Graciously.*) Chawmed. Chawmed.

SYLVIA. (*Bridling.*) This is absurd.

MARY. Modern life is complicated. When you came in I was just telling Miriam—

CRYSTAL. Oh, come along, Sylvia. The lady is tight.

SYLVIA. Mary, when did you begin drinking?

MARY. (*To Crystal.*) Early in the evening, with Mr. Winston. You *know* Mr. Winston, don't you?

CRYSTAL. (*At door.*) I'm afraid I don't.

SYLVIA. Of course you do, Crystal. I introduced you to him. Don't you remember?

CRYSTAL. Oh, yes, at a cocktail party.

MARY. Well, he's in the lobby now, waiting for someone, Mrs. Haines, and drunker than you can possibly imagine. You'd find him very difficult to handle, in front of Stephen. (*Crystal suddenly changes her mind about going into lobby, moves toward washroom.*)

SYLVIA. Crystal, where are you going?

CRYSTAL. I won't stand here and listen to drivel!

MARY. I wouldn't go in there, either, Mrs. Haines. Buck's wife's in there now, having hysterics. She's found out that Buck has been deceiving her.

CRYSTAL. Really! What has that to do with me?

MARY. A good deal, I'm afraid. You seem to be the woman.

SYLVIA. (*Delighted.*) Why, Crystal!—*Are* you?

CRYSTAL. If he used my name, it's a lie! He's just the cheap sort—

MARY. Tomorrow it will be common gossip. I don't think Stephen's going to like it.

SYLVIA. Oh, Crystal, he's going to loathe it! But my psychoanalyst is going to adore it.

CRYSTAL. (*Going to her.*) What are you trying to do? Pin something on me, in front of witnesses?

SYLVIA. Whatever she's driving at, Crystal— (*Pointing to Miriam.*) that little tramp put her up to it!

CRYSTAL. (*To Sylvia.*) Keep out of this!

MIRIAM. Yeah, check it, Sylvia, we're minor league this evening.

CRYSTAL. All right, Mrs. Haines, you've been listening to the ravings of a conceited fool. What did he tell you?

MARY. (*Playing for time, or inspiration.*) Really, Mrs. Haines, this is very embarrassing.

CRYSTAL. (*Brazening it out.*) Yes, Mrs. Haines, isn't it? Exactly what do you think you know about me?

MARY. Everything! (*A pause. Crystal laughs.*)

CRYSTAL. Then why are you standing here talking to me? You ought to be outside spilling it to Stephen. You're bluffing. Come along, Sylvia!

MARY. (*Also moving to door. Crystal stops.*) That's very good advice. I will tell Stephen.

CRYSTAL. Oh, he wouldn't believe you.

SYLVIA. Oh, you can't tell, Crystal! He's terribly fond of Mary.

CRYSTAL. Now get this straight, Mrs. Haines. You handed me your husband on a silver platter. (*Enter Nancy, L.*) But I'm not returning the compliment. I like what I've got and I'm going to keep it. I can't be stampeded by gossip. What you believe and what Stephen believes will cut no ice in a divorce court. You need proof and you haven't got it. When Mr. Winston comes to his senses, he'll apologize. And Stephen will have no choice but to accept my explanations. Now that's that! Good night!

MARY. (*Desperately.*) I hope Mrs. Winston will accept your explanations.

CRYSTAL. What have I got to explain to her?

MARY. (*With a conviction she does not feel.*) What about the apartment?

CRYSTAL. What apartment?

MARY. You know as well as I do.

CRYSTAL. Oh, stop trying to put two and two together—

MARY. Oh, Mrs. Winston did that. She had you watched—she's seen you both.

CRYSTAL. (*Defiantly.*) Seen us both? Doing what?

MARY. Going in, and coming out!

CRYSTAL. Going in and coming out of *where?* (*A pause.*) You're lying!

SYLVIA. (*Warningly.*) I wouldn't be so sure, Crystal!

MIRIAM. Sounds like the McCoy to me, Crystal.

CRYSTAL. Shut up!

SYLVIA. Oh, Crystal, why didn't you confide in me? (*Crystal turns to door again, triumphant.*)

MARY. (*Dismayed.*) Sylvia, didn't she?

SYLVIA. Certainly *not!* (*Crystal smiles, very pleased with herself.*) She's the cat that walks alone. (*Goes to Crystal.*) Why, Crystal, I could have told you some place *much safer* than the Gothic Apartments.

CRYSTAL. (*Exploding.*) Why, you big, loud-mouthed idiot!

SYLVIA. How dare you!

CRYSTAL. I'd like to slap your stupid face.

SYLVIA. (*Backing up.*) How dare you! Oh, Mary, how dare she?

MIRIAM. Oh, I've got a job to do on Flora. (*She pats Sylvia affectionately.*) Kiss you when I get back, Sylvia. (*Exits L.*)

NANCY. And I'll explain the facts of life to Stephen. (*Nancy exits R.*)

CRYSTAL. (*To Mary, fiercely.*) You're trying to break up my marriage!

SYLVIA. The way you did hers, you floosie!

CRYSTAL. (*Nasty.*) Well, maybe you're welcome to my—leftovers.

MARY. (*Calmly.*) I'll take them, thank you.

SYLVIA. Why, Mary, haven't you any *pride?*

MARY. That's right. No, no pride; that's a luxury a woman in love can't afford. (*Enter Countess and Miriam,* L. *Miriam goes to Sadie, gets Countess' and her own wraps.*)

COUNTESS. (*Rushing for Crystal.*) Oh, you—you horse thief!

MARY. (*Stopping her.*) Flora, it's really too bad—

COUNTESS. (*To Crystal.*) You—you painted wagon!

CRYSTAL. So you're determined to have a scandal, Mrs. Haines.

COUNTESS. I'm the one who's going to have the scandal. Why, Mary, she's no more a blonde naturelle than I am. What's the creature's name? Miriam forgot to tell me.

MARY. Mrs. Stephen Haines, currently.

COUNTESS. Is that the thing Stephen left you for? Well, cherie, all I can say is, you're an idiot! I hope I never live to see the day when an obvious piece like that conquers *me* on the champs d'amour! (*She exits,* R., *followed by Miriam.*)

CRYSTAL. (*To Mary.*) You were lying. That old fool didn't know about us. (*Sadie gives Mary her wrap.*)

MARY. I'm afraid she didn't. (*Enter Nancy,* R.)

NANCY. There's a gentleman called Mr. Haines. He says he's been waiting a long time for his wife— (*Crystal moves to get her wrap.*)

MARY. (*Stepping between her and Sadie.*) I am coming. (*Exit Nancy quickly.*)

SYLVIA. Mary, what a dirty female trick you played!

CRYSTAL. Yes! From the great, noble little woman! You're just a cat, like all the rest of us!

MARY. Well, I've had two years to sharpen my claws. (*Waves her hand gaily to Sylvia.*) Jungle Red, Sylvia! Good night, ladies! (*Exits, leaving Crystal and Sylvia alone. As curtain falls, Crystal raises her bag to belt Sylvia, and Sylvia backs fearfully away.*)

OR

CURTAIN FALLS—*Then rises to find Crystal and Sylvia pulling hair.*

PROPERTY LIST

ACT I—SCENE 1

1 magazine
1 silver tea set (tray, creamer, sugar, teapot, hot water pitcher)
1 lace scarf for tray
4 napkins
1 tea set
4 snuffalite ash trays
1 score pad and pencil
2 decks cards
1 table pad

1 cloisonné cigarette box
1 cloisonné ash bowl
1 glass cigarette box
4 cups
4 saucers
1 cake plate
1 sandwich plate
1 padded jacket in box
1 glass ash tray

ACT I—SCENE 2

1 hand mirror
1 blue cotton jar
1 podiatrist case
1 manicure basket (files, etc.)
1 manicure bowl, brush
1 glass ash tray
1 sandwich plate

1 brass ash tray
1 long-handled dust pan
1 long-handled brush
1 special book
2 dozen towels
1 pillow

ACT I—SCENE 3

1 toilet set (brush comb, mirror)
1 bottle astringent
1 box Kleenex
2 small blue bottles
1 glass bowl (glass ice)

1 doily, 1 guest towel
1 blue atomizer
2 blue jars
1 special book

ACT I—SCENE 4

1 sherry glass
2 blue hand mirrors
2 salesladies' books

2 brass ash trays
Blue plush coat hangers

ACT I—SCENE 6

1 carving knife
3 white plates
3 cups and saucers
1 coffeepot and pad

Spoons and forks
1 pie knife
1 sugar bowl
1 vacuum cleaner

ACT I—SCENE 7

1 box orchids

Act II—Scene 1

4 baskets flowers
1 box flowers
1 baby doll
2 baby blankets
3 gift books

1 glass ash tray
1 white French phone
1 letter
2 glass bowls flowers

Act II—Scene 2

2 letters
1 postcard
1 gallon jug (glass)
1 small suitcase
1 large suitcase

1 light steamer trunk
1 Bakelite tray
1 thermos pitcher
5 glasses
3 brass ash trays

Act II—Scene 3

4 bath sheets
4 bath towels
1 hotel key
Hairpins, boxes, etc.
1 toilet bottle set
1 large vanity
1 bottle toilet water
1 lipstick
1 bottle hair bleach
1 bottle Colyrium
2 jars cold cream
1 bottle bath salts
1 toilet set
1 cut glass set

1 square glass powder
1 large powder puff
1 soap bowl
1 gold telephone
1 complexion brush
1 cake soap
2 bath cloths
1 glass ash tray
1 magazine
1 pink sponge
1 glass bowl
1 sherry glass
1 wine glass
1 bath bubble effect

Act II—Scene 4

1 small book
1 covered box matches
1 silver tray

2 cigarette boxes
3 cigarette trays
2 highball glasses

Act II—Scene 5

1 filled cigarette tray
1 water glass, spoon
1 bottle bromo-seltzer
12 velour hangers (red)

1 sewing kit
Hat checks
2 brass ash trays

NEW PLAYS

★ **THE EXONERATED by Jessica Blank and Erik Jensen.** Six interwoven stories paint a picture of an American criminal justice system gone horribly wrong and six brave souls who persevered to survive it. "The #1 play of the year...intense and deeply affecting..." *–NY Times.* "Riveting. Simple, honest storytelling that demands reflection." *–A.P.* "Artful and moving...pays tribute to the resilience of human hearts and minds." *–Variety.* "Stark...riveting...cunningly orchestrated." *–The New Yorker.* "Hard-hitting, powerful, and socially relevant." *–Hollywood Reporter.* [7M, 3W] ISBN: 0-8222-1946-8

★ **STRING FEVER by Jacquelyn Reingold.** Lily juggles the big issues: turning forty, artificial insemination and the elusive scientific Theory of Everything in this Off-Broadway comedy hit. "Applies the elusive rules of string theory to the conundrums of one woman's love life. Think *Sex and the City* meets *Copenhagen.*" *–NY Times.* "A funny offbeat and touching look at relationships...an appealing romantic comedy populated by oddball characters." *–NY Daily News.* "Where kooky, zany, and madcap meet...whimsically winsome." *–NY Magazine.* "STRING FEVER will have audience members happily stringing along." *–TheaterMania.com.* "Reingold's language is surprising, inventive, and unique." *–nytheatre.com.* "...[a] whimsical comic voice." *–Time Out.* [3M, 3W (doubling)] ISBN: 0-8222-1952-2

★ **DEBBIE DOES DALLAS adapted by Erica Schmidt, composed by Andrew Sherman, conceived by Susan L. Schwartz.** A modern morality tale told as a comic musical of tragic proportions as the classic film is brought to the stage. "A scream! A saucy, tongue-in-cheek romp." *–The New Yorker.* "Hilarious! DEBBIE manages to have it all: beauty, brains and a great sense of humor!" *–Time Out.* "Shamelessly silly, shrewdly self-aware and proud of being naughty. Great fun!" *–NY Times.* "Racy and raucous, a lighthearted, fast-paced thoroughly engaging and hilarious send-up." *–NY Daily News.* [3M, 5W] ISBN: 0-8222-1955-7

★ **THE MYSTERY PLAYS by Roberto Aguirre-Sacasa.** Two interrelated one acts, loosely based on the tradition of the medieval mystery plays. "... stylish, spine-tingling...Mr. Aguirre-Sacasa uses standard tricks of horror stories, borrowing liberally from masters like Kafka, Lovecraft, Hitchcock...But his mastery of the genre is his own...irresistible." *–NY Times.* "Undaunted by the special-effects limitations of theatre, playwright and *Marvel* comic-book writer Roberto Aguirre-Sacasa maps out some creepy twilight zones in THE MYSTERY PLAYS, an engaging, related pair of one acts...The theatre may rarely deliver shocks equivalent to, say, *Dawn of the Dead,* but Aguirre-Sacasa's work is fine compensation." *–Time Out.* [4M, 2W] ISBN: 0-8222-2038-5

★ **THE JOURNALS OF MIHAIL SEBASTIAN by David Auburn.** This epic one-man play spans eight tumultuous years and opens a uniquely personal window on the Romanian Holocaust and the Second World War. "Powerful." *–NY Times.* "[THE JOURNALS OF MIHAIL SEBASTIAN] allows us to glimpse the idiosyncratic effects of that awful history on one intelligent, pragmatic, recognizably real man..." *–NY Newsday.* [3M, 5W] ISBN: 0-8222-2006-7

★ **LIVING OUT by Lisa Loomer.** The story of the complicated relationship between a Salvadoran nanny and the Anglo lawyer she works for. "A stellar new play. Searingly funny." *–The New Yorker.* "Both generous and merciless, equally enjoyable and disturbing." *–NY Newsday.* "A bitingly funny new comedy. The plight of working mothers is explored from two pointedly contrasting perspectives in this sympathetic, sensitive new play." *–Variety.* [2M, 6W] ISBN: 0-8222-1994-8

DRAMATISTS PLAY SERVICE, INC.
440 Park Avenue South, New York, NY 10016 212-683-8960 Fax 212-213-1539
postmaster@dramatists.com www.dramatists.com

NEW PLAYS

★ **MATCH by Stephen Belber.** Mike and Lisa Davis interview a dancer and choreographer about his life, but it is soon evident that their agenda will either ruin or inspire them— and definitely change their lives forever. "Prolific laughs and ear-to-ear smiles." —*NY Magazine.* "Uproariously funny, deeply moving, enthralling theater. Stephen Belber's MATCH has great beauty and tenderness, and abounds in wit." —*NY Daily News.* "Three and a half out of four stars." —*USA Today.* "A theatrical steeplechase that leads straight from outrageous bitchery to unadorned, heartfelt emotion." —*Wall Street Journal.* [2M, 1W] ISBN: 0-8222-2020-2

★ **HANK WILLIAMS: LOST HIGHWAY by Randal Myler and Mark Harelik.** The story of the beloved and volatile country-music legend Hank Williams, featuring twenty-five of his most unforgettable songs. "[LOST HIGHWAY has] the exhilarating feeling of Williams on stage in a particular place on a particular night…serves up classic country with the edges raw and the energy hot…By the end of the play, you've traveled on a profound emotional journey: LOST HIGHWAY transports its audience and communicates the inspiring message of the beauty and richness of Williams' songs…forceful, clear-eyed, moving, impressive." —*Rolling Stone.* "…honors a very particular musical talent with care and energy… smart, sweet, poignant." —*NY Times.* [7M, 3W] ISBN: 0-8222-1985-9

★ **THE STORY by Tracey Scott Wilson.** An ambitious black newspaper reporter goes against her editor to investigate a murder and finds the *best* story…but at what cost? "A singular new voice…deeply emotional, deeply intellectual, and deeply musical…" —*The New Yorker.* "…a conscientious and absorbing new drama…" —*NY Times.* "…a riveting, tough-minded drama about race, reporting and the truth…" —*A.P.* "… a stylish, attention-holding script that ends on a chilling note that will leave viewers with much to talk about." —*Curtain Up.* [2M, 7W (doubling, flexible casting)] ISBN: 0-8222-1998-0

★ **OUR LADY OF 121st STREET by Stephen Adly Guirgis.** The body of Sister Rose, beloved Harlem nun, has been stolen, reuniting a group of life-challenged childhood friends who square off as they wait for her return. "A scorching and dark new comedy… Mr. Guirgis has one of the finest imaginations for dialogue to come along in years." —*NY Times.* "Stephen Guirgis may be the best playwright in America under forty." —*NY Magazine.* [8M, 4W] ISBN: 0-8222-1965-4

★ **HOLLYWOOD ARMS by Carrie Hamilton and Carol Burnett.** The coming-of-age story of a dreamer who manages to escape her bleak life and follow her romantic ambitions to stardom. Based on Carol Burnett's bestselling autobiography, *One More Time.* "…pure theatre and pure entertainment…" —*Talkin' Broadway.* "…a warm, fuzzy evening of theatre." —*BrodwayBeat.com.* "…chuckles and smiles of recognition or surprise flow naturally…a remarkable slice of life." —*TheatreScene.net.* [5M, 5W, 1 girl] ISBN: 0-8222-1959-X

★ **INVENTING VAN GOGH by Steven Dietz.** A haunting and hallucinatory drama about the making of art, the obsession to create and the fine line that separates truth from myth. "Like a van Gogh painting, Dietz's story is a gorgeous example of excess—one that remakes reality with broad, well-chosen brush strokes. At evening's end, we're left with the author's resounding opinions on art and artifice, and provoked by his constant query into which is greater: van Gogh's art or his violent myth." —*Phoenix New Times.* "Dietz's writing is never simple. It is always brilliant. Shaded, compressed, direct, lucid—he frames his subject with a remarkable understanding of painting as a physical experience." —*Tucson Citizen.* [4M, 1W] ISBN: 0-8222-1954-9

DRAMATISTS PLAY SERVICE, INC.
440 Park Avenue South, New York, NY 10016 212-683-8960 Fax 212-213-1539
postmaster@dramatists.com www.dramatists.com

NEW PLAYS

★ **INTIMATE APPAREL by Lynn Nottage.** The moving and lyrical story of a turn-of-the-century black seamstress whose gifted hands and sewing machine are the tools she uses to fashion her dreams from the whole cloth of her life's experiences. "…Nottage's play has a delicacy and eloquence that seem absolutely right for the time she is depicting…" *–NY Daily News.* "…thoughtful, affecting…The play offers poignant commentary on an era when the cut and color of one's dress—and of course, skin—determined whom one could and could not marry, sleep with, even talk to in public." *–Variety.* [2M, 4W] ISBN: 0-8222-2009-1

★ **BROOKLYN BOY by Donald Margulies.** A witty and insightful look at what happens to a writer when his novel hits the bestseller list. "The characters are beautifully drawn, the dialogue sparkles…" *–nytheatre.com.* "Few playwrights have the mastery to smartly investigate so much through a laugh-out-loud comedy that combines the vintage subject matter of successful writer-returning-to-ethnic-roots with the familiar mid-life crisis." *–Show Business Weekly.* [4M, 3W] ISBN: 0-8222-2074-1

★ **CROWNS by Regina Taylor.** Hats become a springboard for an exploration of black history and identity in this celebratory musical play. "Taylor pulls off a Hat Trick: She scores thrice, turning CROWNS into an artful amalgamation of oral history, fashion show, and musical theater…" *–TheatreMania.com.* "…wholly theatrical…Ms. Taylor has created a show that seems to arise out of spontaneous combustion, as if a bevy of department-store customers simultaneously decided to stage a revival meeting in the changing room." *–NY Times.* [1M, 6W (2 musicians)] ISBN: 0-8222-1963-8

★ **EXITS AND ENTRANCES by Athol Fugard.** The story of a relationship between a young playwright on the threshold of his career and an aging actor who has reached the end of his. "[Fugard] can say more with a single line than most playwrights convey in an entire script…Paraphrasing the title, it's safe to say this drama, making its memorable entrance into our consciousness, is unlikely to exit as long as a theater exists for exceptional work." *–Variety.* "A thought-provoking, elegant and engrossing new play…" *–Hollywood Reporter.* [2M] ISBN: 0-8222-2041-5

★ **BUG by Tracy Letts.** A thriller featuring a pair of star-crossed lovers in an Oklahoma City motel facing a bug invasion, paranoia, conspiracy theories and twisted psychological motives. "…obscenely exciting…top-flight craftsmanship. Buckle up and brace yourself…" *–NY Times.* "…[a] thoroughly outrageous and thoroughly entertaining play…the possibility of enemies, real and imagined, to squash has never been more theatrical." *–A.P.* [3M, 2W] ISBN: 0-8222-2016-4

★ **THOM PAIN (BASED ON NOTHING) by Will Eno.** An ordinary man muses on childhood, yearning, disappointment and loss, as he draws the audience into his last-ditch plea for empathy and enlightenment. "It's one of those treasured nights in the theater—treasured nights anywhere, for that matter—that can leave you both breathless with exhilaration and…in a puddle of tears." *–NY Times.* "Eno's words…are familiar, but proffered in a way that is constantly contradictory to our expectations. Beckett is certainly among his literary ancestors." *–nytheatre.com.* [1M] ISBN: 0-8222-2076-8

★ **THE LONG CHRISTMAS RIDE HOME by Paula Vogel.** Past, present and future collide on a snowy Christmas Eve for a troubled family of five. "…[a] lovely and hauntingly original family drama…a work that breathes so much life into the theater." *–Time Out.* "…[a] delicate visual feast…" *–NY Times.* "…brutal and lovely…the overall effect is magical." *–NY Newsday.* [3M, 3W] ISBN: 0-8222-2003-2

DRAMATISTS PLAY SERVICE, INC.
440 Park Avenue South, New York, NY 10016   212-683-8960   Fax 212-213-1539
postmaster@dramatists.com   www.dramatists.com